TABLE OF CONTENTS

Page

ACRONYMS

AFP   Armed Forces of the Philippine

ASG   Abu Sayyaf Group

BATT   British Army Training Team

CAT   Civil Action Teams

CMO   Civil Military Operations

COIN   Counterinsurgency

CT   Communist Terrorist

GIROA   Government of the Islamic Republic of Afghanistan

ISAF   International Security Assistance Force

JSOTF-P   Joint Special Operations Forces-Philippines

MCP   Malayan Communist Party

MILF   Moro Islamic Liberation Front

MNLF   Moro National Liberation Front

MPAJA   Malayan Peoples Anti Japanese Army

MRLA   Malayan Races Liberation Army

NATO   North Atlantic Treaty Organization

PDRY   Peoples Democratic Republic of Yemen

PFLOAG   Popular Front for the Liberation of the Occupied Arab Gulf

PRT   Provincial Reconstruction Team

SAF   Sultan of Oman Armed Forces

SAS   Special Air Service

SOF   Special Operations Forces

UNAMA   United Nations Assistance Mission in Afghanistan

USAID   U.S. Agency for International Development

WWII   World War II

ILLUSTRATIONS

TABLES

CHAPTER 1

INTRODUCTION

When we speak about hearts and minds, we are not talking about being nice to the natives, but about giving them a firm smack of government. Hearts and minds denoted authority, not appeasement.[1]
— Hew Strachan

At the core of United States (US) counterinsurgency doctrine is the concept of "hearts and minds."[2] Although the concept has significantly deviated from its historical grounding and seemingly has become a nebulous concept frequently maligned, misunderstood, and misapplied, nonetheless its original principles remain the cornerstone in current counterinsurgency campaigns. The US military is currently engaged in or supporting counterinsurgency campaigns with host nation governments in Iraq, Afghanistan, southern Philippines, and the Horn of Africa. It is necessary for these host nation governments' to win their people's hearts and minds. However, despite the significance of hearts and minds, the concept is often treated as a buzzword--a phrase that is taken at face value with little analysis, historical grounding, or precise understanding of what it entails. Its application also differs in every conflict and periods in history. This thesis looks at the concept of hearts and minds from a historical perspective with the goal of deepening the understanding of the concept and its relevance to contemporary counterinsurgency campaigns.[3] It will examine hearts and minds from three angles. First, is to examine the evolution of the hearts and minds approach from its historical grounding in counterinsurgency. Second, to identify theoretical and field application challenges related to this evolution based on modernization and legitimacy. Lastly, is to provide insights to new and evolving methods in winning hearts and minds. It will offer

1

recommendations to leveraging foreign cultures and delve into the advantage of leveraging religion in the battle for hearts-and-minds; or in this case, applying a hearts and souls approach.

Evolution of the Term Hearts and Minds

Field Marshal Sir Gerald Walter Robert Templer[4] is widely credited for the term hearts and minds when during the Malayan Emergency he said, "The answer lies not in pouring more troops into the jungle, but in the heart and minds of the Malayan People."[5] This approach is contentiously credited for the British/Malayan administration's victory in conflict. In the political arena, the term hearts and minds have been frequently included in American presidents' lexicon. In fact, its first recorded usage predates that of Templer's statement. On 13 February 1818 founding father and America's second President John Adams wrote to a Baltimore newspaper editor and argues:

> The [American] Revolution was affected before the War commenced. The Revolution was in the *minds and hearts* of the people; a change in their religious sentiments of their duties and obligations. This radical change in the principles, opinions, sentiments, and affections of the people, was the real American Revolution.[6]

In the thick of the Cold War, hearts and minds crept into US counterrevolutionary rhetoric. President John F. Kennedy, on 2 April 1963, tells Congress, "Perhaps most significant of all is a change in the hearts and minds of the people - a growing will to develop their countries. We can only help Latin Americans to save themselves."[7] On 14 September 2005, to bring international credence to Operation Iraqi Freedom, President George W. Bush justified the invasion by hailing the possibility of a political transformation of the Middle East, telling the U.N. General Assembly, "Across the world, hearts and minds are opening to the message of human liberty as never before."[8] Even the

2

current U.S. President Barack Obama used the phrase in his campaign to reset relations with both the Muslim world and Russia in 9 January 2009, "[Abiding by the Geneva Conventions] . . . will make us safer and will help in changing hearts and minds in our struggle against extremists," and once again in Moscow six months later, "[By] mobilizing and organizing and changing people's hearts and minds, you then change the political landscape."[9]

However, it was during the Vietnam War that hearts and minds was introduced to the American public through mass media that left an indelible mark and associated the phrase to a lofty and an untenable goal. On 4 May 1965 U.S. President Lyndon B. Johnson said, "ultimate victory [in Vietnam] will depend upon the hearts and the minds of the Vietnamese."[10] But the policy did not match the rhetoric. The counterinsurgency campaign launched by the South Vietnamese, with intial American passive support, was more brutal than any previous campaigns even compared with Malaya. The approach to the war included the strategic hamlet program (forcefully moving villagers into guarded camps); poisoning the rice crop; assassination campaigns (including the Phoenix program which set a monthly quota of guerrillas to be neutralized); saturation bombing; and designating free-fire zones where anything living was presumed to be hostile.[11] Unlike most of these covert operations in Vietnam, in Malaya the British/Malayan administration was savvy to first proclaim Emergency regulations before repressive actions were forcefully executed. This insured that the government's actions were justified and conducted within the law.

The 1974 Academy Award-winning Vietnam documentary, *Hearts and Minds,*[12] cemented the phrase's negative connotations in the American psyche. US politicians and military commanders adopted the phrase hearts and minds to describe their approach to counterinsurgency in Vietnam, but the phrase concealed the reality of a far more conventional and coercive approach to counterinsurgency. Referring to the war effort, Richard Stubbs argues, the US military associated the hearts and minds approach with coercive tactics, such as "search and destroy," which were more forceful than the policies followed in Malaya, partly due to the fact the war in Vietnam was different and the enemy was stronger and more violent. [13] The enemy had a conventional and insurgent structure. In frustration, Templer in 1968 referred to hearts and minds as, "that nauseating phrase I think I invented."[14] The disdain for its ill-application in counterinsurgency by those who favored a conventional solution to the Vietnam conflict is captured best by an unknown Army officer who said, "grab em by the balls and their hearts and minds will follow."[15] Consequently, since that humiliating defeat, hearts and minds has had minimal attention in U.S. doctrine.

During the first decade of the 21st century, the US military experienced a counterinsurgency renaissance that ushered in the resurgence of the term hearts and minds. The U.S. launched two major campaigns and seemingly attained quick victories in both Operation Enduring Freedom-Afghanistan (2001) and Operation Iraqi Freedom (2003) only to realize that the victories were not final. America was drawn into unfamiliar and protracted conflicts. Although the US military defeated all organized resistance by the Iraqi Army and the Taliban, resistance evolved into an insurgency. These precarious situations revived the interest in counterinsurgency.

Hearts and minds is a much criticized and controversial counterinsurgency approach that is least examined yet evokes strong opinions and emotions. In clear contrast to the reliance on military solutions in conventional wars, counterinsurgency theory and practice emphasize full spectrum warfare. The goal of counterinsurgency is to gain legitimacy for the government of the host nation; this means that the support of the populace, on which the legitimacy of governing institutions rests, is required. While previous successful counterinsurgency campaigns will not produce a template for today, the sum of these experiences when viewed through judicious and analytical lenses will portray a recurring theme in counterinsurgency. Chief of which is the importance of winning the hearts and minds of the population in order to gain their allegiance away from insurgents. This counterinsurgency approach is often seen as a response to the success of Mao Zedong's guerrilla warfare in China in 1949. Mao emphasized winning the hearts and minds of the people, he famously commented, "The guerrilla must move amongst the people as a fish swims in the sea" therefore, to counter Mao, "Dry up the sea, or drain the swamp, through a hearts and minds campaign and the fish die. However, he contradicted himself as well with, "Political power grows out of the barrel of a gun."[16]

The primary goal of a counterinsurgency operation is to protect/control the population in order to obtain its tacit and active support in putting down the insurgency and thereby gain its allegiance. Winning the people's hearts and minds is the key to counterinsurgents' victory. Unlike the conventional warfare model that is primarily oriented on the destruction of the enemy or controlling key terrain, in counterinsurgency controlling the population is the focus. Kilcullen highlights the primacy of the population over terrain and the enemy in counterinsurgency:

> The enemy needs the people to act in certain ways - sympathy, acquiescence, silence, provocation - and without these insurgents wither. The enemy is fluid and the population is fixed; therefore, controlling the population is

5

a better option than destroying the enemy. Being fluid, the enemy can control his loss rate. The enemy will pick his time and place of battle. They can never be eradicated by attrition alone. In any given area, there are multiple threat groups but only one local population. Since the enemy conceals himself within the human terrain,[17] the enemy might not be identifiable but the population is.[18]

The prevailing misunderstanding and the ambiguity surrounding the hearts and minds concept is rooted from its inception and implementation during the Malayan Emergency. Templer, once again with reference to Malaya, states, "The shooting side of business is only 25 percent of the trouble and the other 75 percent is getting the people of this country behind us."[19] This statement coupled with his most popular, "The answer lies not in pouring more troops into the jungle, but in the heart and minds of the Malayan People,"[20] mistakenly associated hearts and minds to only a kinder and gentler or softer approach when dealing with the civilian population but nothing could be farther from the truth. On the contrary, the British applied highly coercive methods in Malaya. Paul Dixon argues that our understanding of past counterinsurgency successes may be flawed and that the operations during the colonial withdrawal were actually much more violent and coercive.[21] Moreover, he highlights the fact that, historically, there were many interpretations of the phrase hearts and minds, which also lead to confusion about what degree of consent should be expected from the people and the implication of this for the use of force.[22] Those who wish merely to win the acquiescence, respect, toleration or fear of the population may believe that this is possible even with the use of much higher levels of violence and that this had been the recipe for success in the British Empire.[23] By way of example, Strachan makes a far more coercive interpretation of the historical approach to winning hearts and minds, "When we speak about hearts and minds, we are not talking about being nice to the natives, but about giving them a firm smack of government.

6

Hearts and minds denoted authority, not appeasement. Of course, political and social reform might accompany firm government."[24]

Approaching with lesser emphasis on coercion, Thomas Mockaitis[25] articulates the significance of addressing material grievances. In essence, he advocates taking the revolution from the revolutionaries. He asserts:

> Winning hearts and minds has become a much maligned and often misunderstood concept that conjures up images of soldiers building playgrounds for smiling children, diverting personnel and resources from their proper task of fighting wars. A hearts and minds campaign, however, consists of soberly assessing what motivates people to rebel and devising a strategy to address the underlying causes of unrest. In most cases discontent stems from bread-and-butter issues. Lack of jobs, decent housing, electricity, running water, health care, and education can motivate people to accept or even actively support insurgents. He contends, people generally support an insurgency out of a shared sense of wrong or frustration at not having their basic needs met.[26]

In order to gain the population's support, counterinsurgent forces must recognize and address the needs and the legitimate grievances of the local population. It is on this that insurgency thrives. Mockaitis continues with, "Once their basic needs have been met, however, people may desire political freedoms, the absence of which can also fuel an insurgency."[27] He addresses the "heart" aspect but marginalized the significance of engaging the "mind." Political will is necessary to win "the battle for hearts and minds" of the affected population because only if the people believe that the government will win can they be drawn away from the insurgent's cause. If the people think the government will lose, then they may well throw in their lot with their future masters--the insurgents.[28]

From Coercion to Contemporary Modernization and Legitimacy

As revealed from the classical counterinsurgency era writings of, David Galula, Sir Frank Edward Kitson, and Sir Robert Thompson, the application of hearts and minds is a combination of coercion and consent with a heavier dose of the former to influence and control the population's behavior. As the mindset is being changed, small acts of support (e.g. medical and veterinary support) and the way in which government security forces interact with the population, combined with an effective information operations campaign, wins over their hearts.[29] The current counterinsurgency renaissance has redefined this approach in order to suit the political correctness and media advancements of our time. Current methods must conform to the current interpretation of human rights and justice within the realm of 24-hour news media. The balance is now tilted in favor of more consent building than coercion. With this paradigm shift, the insurgent has an advantage. He can use violence, intimidation, and terror to coerce support from the population and does not need to be everywhere all the time. He only has to present a credible threat once in order to coerce support. The counterinsurgent on the other hand has to be everywhere all the time and has to be able to continuously protect the population in order to win their loyalty and support.[30] The term "courageous restrain"[31] highlights this disadvantage since a majority of the coercive tools of the past that allowed the physical "draining of the sea" can no longer be applied.

Today, the execution of hearts and minds is based on modernization and legitimacy. The intellectual foundations of this new approach are grounded in the modernization theory and a legal legitimacy coupled with a "force for good" narrative within the normative state-building and democratization agendas of operations.[32] The new approach to winning the "heart" is aligned with the modernization theory. The theory is based on the purposeful development of societies through several stages of modernization from primitive traditional forms toward Western-style industrialization, secularization, and political pluralism.[33] It looks at the internal factors of a country while assuming that, with assistance, "traditional" countries can be brought to development in the same manner more developed Western countries have. It attempts to identify the social variables which contribute to social progress and development of societies, and seeks to explain the process of social evolution. The theory not only stresses the process of change but also the responses to that change, and also looks at internal dynamics while referring to social and cultural structures and the adaptation of new technologies. However, the very Western approach to modernization is not always viewed favorably in every culture. It could serve as a friction point, a source of conflict with other culture for it views traditions as obstacles to economic growth. Furthermore, even if it causes violent and radical change to traditional societies, it was thought worthy of the price.

Modernization's critics insist that traditional societies were often destroyed without ever gaining promised advantages if, among other things, the economic gap between advanced societies and such societies actually increased. The net effect of modernization for some societies was therefore the replacement of traditional poverty by a more modern form of misery.[34] A society will never miss something it never had. It will remain comfortable with the familiar or the restoration of what was previously known. For instance, the internet is never missed by someone who has always used a radio and never tried the information superhighway. The familiar transistor radio will always suffice. Quite a small price to pay if maintaining the traditional ways is the highest societal aspiration.

As to the new approach to winning the "mind," it is reliant on establishing legitimacy and much less reliant to application of coercion. Michael Fitzsimmons asserts:

9

The premise of most Western thinking on counterinsurgency is that success depends on establishing a perception of legitimacy for the ruling regime among some critical portion of the local population. Among the mechanisms available to counterinsurgents for establishing that legitimacy, one of the most prominent in both practice and doctrine has been the improvement of governance in the form of effective and efficient administration of government and public services. Good governance, by this logic, is the key to "winning hearts and minds."[35]

More specifically, the foundation of counterinsurgency strategy has its roots in the legal-rational conception of Western political legitimacy. This very parochial Western view could prove damaging to efforts in Afghanistan.[36] Other theorists view legitimacy as nothing more and nothing less than the right to rule or a popular perception or belief in legitimacy. Thus, Max Weber in his book *Economy and Society* enumerates a number of different forms of legitimate authority. First, there is charismatic authority, based on the charisma of the leader, often implying certain extra or religious attributes. Second, traditional authority based on custom of the past or habit. Third, the rational-legal authority with legitimacy based on the perception that a government's powers are derived from set procedures, principles, and laws.[37] The first and second examples do not always entail a one man, one vote concept that dominates Western political legitimacy.

Conclusively, this contemporary and less coercive hearts and minds approach based on modernization and legitimacy is not without challenges, foremost of which stems from a disconnect between its Western-centric foundation for legitimacy and development and its implementation in foreign cultures. As for winning the hearts through modernization, the conventional approach to counterinsurgency advocates the need to address the needs and the legitimate grievances of the local population in order to win them away from the insurgents. However, the counterinsurgent familiarization to modernity has meant that they have had preconceived ideas about what needs and

10

grievances to address rather than to actually listen to the local population. The aims of

these operations indicate that it is not any type of governance or reform that is being

supported by external counterinsurgents. It is a very specific. Western set of norms that

are being introduced or reinforced--regardless of the local wishes or perceived needs. If a

counterinsurgents unit assesses that a village needs a school even if the local elders are

asking to have their mosque repaired, a school is built.[38] How much rapport and influence

do you think the counterinsurgent forces made? We must avoid building little Americas

and view the world through a purely Western prism.

As to winning "minds" through legitimacy, the narrow interpretation of

legitimacy that is bounded by the Jeffersonian democratic concepts not only subjects

other activities in vain, but may also be counterproductive. Instead, a broader

understanding of legitimacy and the way it operates within the specific culture, such as

Afghanistan, is necessary in order to create informed strategies, and possibly lowered

expectation. The significant challenge here is whether the international community can

adjust towards anything different from its concepts of legitimacy, good governance, and

development. The traditional sources of legitimacy in other cultures often based on

identity, tribal customs, or cultural affinity, produces a dilemma for Western policy

makers. Their sense of equality and one-man, one-vote concepts is instead imposed. The

result is a steep uphill battle for legitimacy that is therefore unlikely to be won by

incremental improvements in the economic and social situation. This situation spirals to

instability and the failure to provide the most basic services of security and justice;

thereby, eroding legitimacy. Interviewed Dhofar veterans expressed, "We laughed when

we heard that the coalition is holding elections in Afghanistan. They are similar to the

Dhofaris who had an existing tribal political system."[39] We must accept the local system of governance and justice instead of changing and infusing an unfamiliar model. The establishment of Western norms of governance and certain tactical efforts to win the hearts and minds of the local population, at its worst, could initiate a crisis of legitimacy if it starts out by tearing down traditional power structures consequently threatening the power and status of existing powerbrokers.[40]

The primary focus of counterinsurgency operations should therefore be to improve the performance and legitimacy of multiple indigenous actors. Only they can win their people's hearts and minds. Seth Jones accurately argues that improving indigenous governance and performance includes "improving the quality of the police and other security forces, strengthening governance capacity, and undermining external support for insurgents."[41] Additionally, the use of internal forces taking a leading role can provide a focus for national aspirations and show the population that they--and not foreign forces--control their destiny.[42]

In *Political Man*, Seymor Martin Lipset argues that the stability of a political system is determined by its decision making effectiveness and the legitimacy of the political system. Effectiveness refers to the actual performance of the system in terms of satisfying the basic functions of government as the majority of the population in the state perceives them.[43] He emphasizes that legitimacy stems from the political system's ability to create and maintain a popular belief in the existing political system and a perception of the system's institutions as the best suited to the particular society. It is the perception of effectiveness and suitability that is important--not "objective" measures of legality and rationality. Moreover, legitimacy is a question of values by which different groups in

12

society would perceive the system as legitimate or illegitimate based on how well their own values matched with that of the system.

Legitimacy is thereby inherently subjective. Importantly, while effectiveness is largely instrumental, legitimacy is inherently evaluative in that the population regards a political system legitimate or illegitimate according to the way in which its values fit with theirs.[44] These views on legitimacy are significant as they imply that if the main objective really is to win hearts and minds through legitimacy, reforms and activities should ideally imitate existing values and perceptions of legitimate governance rather than the current focus on Western, liberal norms of governance.[45]

This thesis is organized into five chapters. Chapter 1 introduces the topic hearts and minds: its history, evolution, significance to counterinsurgency, and its current manifestation based on modernization and legitimacy. Chapter 2 consists of a literature review of the theory and doctrine dealing with hearts and minds and a brief review of the literature pertinent to each of the four cases studies. Chapter 3 discusses the methodology used for research. This thesis used comparative case studies and relied upon conducted oral history interviews to explore the perception and application of hearts and minds. Chapter 4 demonstrates how the research results surrounding the case studies help address the issues presented above, such as the effectiveness of hearts and minds, successful but highly coercive methods historically applied, and the evolution of new methods in persecuting current campaigns. Finally, Chapter 5 concludes the thesis and includes recommendations for counterinsurgency campaign planners. Most significant would be the final assessment of wither hearts and minds merits continued consideration and implementation or simply left in history's dustbin.

[1]Hew Strachan, "British Counter-Insurgency from Malaya to Iraq," *Royal United Services Institute Journal* 152, no. 6 (December. 2007): 8.

[2]Strategic Studies Department, *United States Special Operations Command (USSOCOM) Research Topic 2010* (Hurlburt, FL, Joint Special Operations University, 2009), 16.

[3]Ibid.

[4]Field Marshal Sir Gerald Walter Robert Templer was a British military commander best known for his defeat of the guerrilla rebels in Malaya between 1952 and 1954. Winston Churchill appointed him British High Commissioner in Malaya in January 1952. Enhancing General Sir Harold Briggs strategy against the communists (Briggs' Plan), Templer's effort is considered as a model for counterinsurgency. He demanded that newly built villages, where ethnic Chinese were resettled away from the jungles and beyond the reach (and influence) of the guerrillas, look inviting in order to gain the "hearts and minds" of the non-Malays (Chinese population), who were the main source of communist support. When he left Malaya the situation was dramatically improved, though the rebels remained a force. "The jungle has been neutralized," he declared in a Time Magazine cover article in 1952.

[5]John Cloake, *Templer: Tiger of Malaya. The Life of Field Marshal Sir Gerald Templer* (London: Harrap Publishing, 1985), 262.

[6]Sydney E. Ahlstrom and David D. Hall, *A Religious History of the American People* (New Haven CT: Yale University Press, 2004), 262.

[7]Robert A. Goldwin and John Fitzgerald Kennedy, *Why Foreign Aid?* (Manchester NH: Ayer Publishing, 1971), 139.

[8]Elizabeth Dickinson, "A Bright Shining Slogan How 'Hearts and Minds' Came to Be," *Foreign Policy* (September/October 2009), http://www.foreignpolicy.com/articles/2009/08/13/a_bright_shining_slogan (accessed 10 October 2010).

[9]Ibid.

[10]Ibid.

[11]Marilyn B. Young, *Counterinsurgency, Now and Forever and Lloyd C. Gardner, Iraq and the Lessons of Vietnam: Or, How Not to Learn from the Past* (New York: The New Press 2007).

[12]"Hearts and Minds," a 1974 Academy Award winning documentary of the conflicting attitudes of the opponents of the Vietnam war. This film recounts the history and attitudes of the opposing sides of the Vietnam War using archival news footage as

well as their own film and interviews. A key theme is how attitudes of American racism and self-righteousness militarism helped create and prolong this bloody conflict.

[13]Richard Stubbs, *Hearts and Minds in Guerrilla Warfare: Malayan Emergency, 1948-60* (Oxford: Oxford University Press, 1989), 3.

[14]Ibid., 1.

[15]There is no definitive source for the quote, different literatures attribute the phrase from President Johnson, General Westmoreland, General James Hollingsworth (Cdr, 1st Infantry Div in Vietnam) to "an Army Officer" in Vietnam.

[16]Mao Tse-Tung, *Selected Works, Vol. II* (New York: International Publishers, 1954), 272.

[17]Human Terrain lacks a common definition but its use is widespread among current counterinsurgency theorists and practitioners. Borrowing from the British Army's Afghan Counterinsurgency Centre's working definition, "it is the social, political, and economic environment, belief systems and forms of interaction of the people among whom soldiers operate."

[18]David Kilcullen, "Counterinsurgency in Iraq: Theory and Practice, 2007," Power point presentation, September 2007, http://usacac.army.mil/cac2/coin/.../ Dr_Kilcullen_COIN_Brief%28Sep07%29.ppt (accessed 15 October 2010).

[19]Cloake, *Templer: Tiger of Malaya. The Life of Field Marshal Sir Gerald Templer*, 262.

[20]Ibid.

[21]Paul Dixon, "'Hearts and Minds'? British Counter-Insurgency from Malaya to Iraq," *Journal of Strategic Studies* 32, 3 (June 2009): 366.

[22]Ibid.

[23]Ibid.

[24]Strachan, "British Counter-Insurgency from Malaya to Iraq," 8.

[25]Several of Dr Thomas R. Mockaitis (Ph.D.) published work include: *The "New" Terrorism: Myths and Reality* (2008); *The Iraq War: Learning from the Past, Adapting to the Present, Preparing for the Future* (2007); *CIMIC* [Civil-military Cooperation] and *CT* [Counterterrorism], special issue of *Small Wars and Insurgencies* 17, no. 4 (December 2006); *Grand Strategy in the War on Terrorism*, (2003); *Future of Peace Operations: Old Challenge for a New Century*, (2004); "Winning Hearts and Minds in the War on Terrorism," *Terrorism and Grand Strategy* (2003); "The Future of Terrorism

Studies," Terrorism and Grand Strategy (2003); *Terrorism Past and Present,*" *World Book: Focus on Terrorism* (2003).

[26]Thomas R. Mockaitis, *The "New" Terrorism: Myths and Reality* (Stanford, CA: Stanford University Press, 2008), 21-22.

[27]Thomas R. Mockaitis, *Iraq and the Challenge of Counterinsurgency* (Westport, CT: Praeger Security International, 2008).

[28]Julian Paget, *Counter-Insurgency Campaigning* (London: Faber Publishing, 1967), 168.

[29]Colonel I. A. Rigden (O.B.E.), British Army, "The British Approach to Counter-Insurgency: Myths, Realities, and Strategic Challenge" (Strategy Research Project, US Army War College, Carlisle Barracks, PA, 2008), 12.

[30]Octavian Manea, "Interview with Dr. John Nagl," *Small Wars Journal,* http://smallwarsjournal.com/blog/journal/docs-temp/599-manea.pdf (accessed 1 November 2010).

[31]Courageous Restraint emphasizes the need to take risks, even to the point of risking physical harm, in order to avert damage to the mission. If we can de-escalate a situation, and avoid civilian casualties, even if potentially justifiable under Rules of Engagement for Self-Defense, we stand a much better chance of succeeding in a COIN campaign. Our goal is to earn the faith and the trust of the Afghan people. We believe honoring Courageous Restraint is an important way to support that goal. (ISAF website http://www.isaf.nato.int/en/article/ caat-anaysis-news/honoring-courageous-restraint.html (accessed 15 November 2010).

[32]Robert Egnell, "Winning Legitimacy: A Critical Analysis of Hearts and Minds Approaches in Afghanistan," Paper presented at the annual meeting of the Theory vs. Policy? Connecting Scholars and Practitioners, New Orleans Hilton Riverside Hotel, The Loews New Orleans Hotel, New Orleans, LA, 17 February 2010.

[33]Ibid.

[34]Majid Rahnema, *Quand la misère chasse la pauvreté* (Arles: Actes Sud, 2003), 268.

[35]Michael Fitzsimmons, "Hard Hearts and Open Minds? Governance, Identity and the Intellectual Foundations of Counterinsurgency Strategy," Paper presented at the annual meeting of the ISA's 49th Annual Convention, Bridging Multiple Divides, Hilton San Francisco, CA, 26 March 2008, http://www.allacademic.com/meta/ p252066_index.html (accessed 22 November 2010).

[36]The victorious British SAS in Dhofar realized the significance of traditional legitimacy within the culture and did not introduce or impose a new political system.

[37]Max Weber, *Economy and Society: An Outline of Interpretive Sociology*, Vol. 2 (Berkley, CA: University of California Press, 1978), 212.

[38]A fitting example to this are the Area Coordination Centers (ACCs) built in Sulu with minimum input from the local population. This will be discussed in the Philippines case study.

[39]CGSC Scholars Program 2010, Dhofar Veterans Panel

[40]Egnell, "Winning Legitimacy."

[41]Seth Jones, *Counterinsurgency in Afghanistan,* Rand Counterinsurgency Study, Vol. 4 (Santa Monica, CA: RAND Corporation, 2008), 24.

[42]Ibid., 10-11.

[43]Seymour Martin Lipset, *Political Man: The Social Bases of Politics* (London: Heinemann Publishing, 1983), 77.

[44]Ibid.

[45]Egnell, "Winning Legitimacy."

CHAPTER 2

LITERATURE REVIEW

Hearts and Minds in Doctrine and Theory

Counterinsurgency has become the US Army's new way of war. The principles and ideas that emerged out of the Army's Field Manual 3-24, *Counterinsurgency*, published in late 2006, have become transcendent. The field manual has moved beyond simple Army doctrine for countering insurgencies to become the defining characteristic of the Army's new way of war.[1] It is based on the idea that the population is the center of gravity. However, it paid minimal attention to hearts and minds, provided no explanation to its historical grounding, and offered no guidance to its effective application. Drawn directly from the pages of FM 3-24, hearts and minds is mentioned:

> Once the unit settles into the AO [Area of Operations], its next task is to build trusted networks. This is the true meaning of the phrase "hearts and minds," which comprises two separate components. "Hearts" means persuading people that their best interests are served by counterinsurgents success. "Minds" means convincing them that the force can protect them and that resisting it is pointless. Note that neither concerns whether people like Soldiers and Marines. Calculated self-interest, not emotion, is what counts. Over time, successful trusted networks grow like roots into the populace. They displace enemy networks, which forces enemies into the open, letting military forces seize the initiative and destroy the insurgents.[2]

Regrettably, this explanation is buried at the back pages of the manual, Appendix A, when a greater amplification is necessary. Its true meaning and significance continues to elude a majority of counterinsurgency practitioners.

Malaya

A sizable body of literature dealing with the British counterinsurgency experience in Malaya exists in both academia and general literature. Interest in the British success in the Malayan Emergency rose in recent years. It was drawn heavily for lessons learned by FM 3-24. One of the most definitive works on Malaya that is commonly read by military professionals is John Nagl's *Learning to Eat Soup with a Knife: Counterinsurgency Lessons from Malaya and Vietnam*. The book compares and contrasts the British approach towards insurgency in Malaya to the American style of war in Vietnam, with obvious repercussions for our current problems in Afghanistan and Iraq. Other notable secondary sources include: Richard Stubbs, "From Search and Destroy to Hearts and Minds: The Evolution of British Strategy in Malaya 1948-60," in Daniel Marston and Carter Malkasian (eds.) *Counterinsurgency in Modern Warfare* (2010); Robert Komer, *The Malayan Emergency in Retrospect: Organization of a Successful Counterinsurgency Effort*. Santa Monica: RAND (1972); Daniel Marston, "Lost and Found in the Jungle," in Hew Strachan (ed.), *Big Wars and Small Wars* (2006); and Wade Markel, "Draining the Swamp: The British Strategy of Population Control," *Parameters* (Spring 2006); Brigadier M. C. A. Henniker, *Red Shadow Over Malaya* (1955); Leon Comber, *Malaya's Secret Police 1945-1960: The Role of the Special Branch in the Malayan Emergency*, (2009); and Richard Miers, *Shoot to Kill* (1959).

Dhofar (Oman)

As a little known but largely successful counterinsurgency operation, there is not an abundance of literary sources that deal with Dhofar and several are even out of print. Considered significant to building a knowledge foundation is Tony Jeapes', *SAS: Operation Oman* (1980), which provides essential and very detailed information about the conflict. Furthermore, it discusses some rather interesting observations in relation to the importance of understanding the history, culture and rule of law when conducting counterinsurgency as a foreign power. Another is John Akehurst's, *We Won a War*

(1982) that explains in detail the distinct combat operations carried out in the Dhofar

region. This source furthermore entails a very informative part on the Omani history and

the history background leading to the insurgency. Next, although it is out of print,

Thomas R. Mockaitis', *British Counterinsurgency in the Post Imperial Era* (1995)

provides an overview of the demanding task of winning the hearts and minds of the

Omani people is described in detail. Other relevant sources include: Ian Beckett, "The

British Counter-insurgency Campaign in Dhofar, 1965-1975," in Daniel Marston and

Carter Malkasian (eds.), *Counterinsurgency in Modern Warfare* (2010); Bard O'Neill,

"Revolutionary War in Oman" in *Insurgency in the Modern World* (1980); and Walter

Ladwig III,"Supporting Allies in COIN: Britain and the Dhofar Rebellion," *Small Wars

and Insurgencies*, vol. 19:1, March 2008.

Philippines

Quietly entering its ninth year, there is very minimal literary sources available

regarding US Special Operations Forces (SOF) presence in the Philippines in support of

Operation Enduring Freedom- Philippines (OEF-P). Besides the recently published book

by Frederic P. Miller, Agnes F. Vandome, and John McBrewster (2010), *Enduring

Freedom-Philippines*, a majority of sources are articles written by US service members

formerly assigned in Joint Special Operations Task Force- Philippines (JSOTF-P) and

from oral history interviews. The author offers an extensive first-hand experience for

having deployed twice in support of with JSOTF-P; first as its Civil Military Operations

Chief and second as the Civil Affairs Commander.

Afghanistan

Similar to OEF-P, little definitive literature exists on the hearts and minds strategy in Afghanistan. Most of the available literature consists of articles in the general press. Almost all of these articles relied upon first hand observations by reporters embedded with US military teams that trained Afghan security forces. Press releases are another source of information on the subject. The preponderance of information on hearts and minds come from firsthand accounts of US and British servicemen in Afghanistan and unit after-action reports, although much of this information is classified or otherwise restricted from public release.

Perhaps the biggest challenge was the lack of open source information on the subject. Since the conflict is ongoing, much of the information on hearts and minds methodology is classified, either due to its content or the medium on which the information is handled (i.e., on a secure internet system). Additionally, because Coalition forces are still fighting the insurgency at the time of writing, it is too early to discern the effectiveness of the US-led coalition effort.

Summary

The aforementioned literature review depicts several trends. First, current US doctrine pays little attention to hearts and minds. However, in current counterinsurgency campaigns, winning the populations hearts and minds (mainly through civil-military operations) is used as a major line of operation. The methods applied by counterinsurgents varied according to periods in history, resources available, and the balance between coercion and persuasion applied. As chapter 4 will show, the British devoted a considerable amount of coercion during the Malayan Emergency while minimal coercion was applied in Dhofar a decade later. In the southern Philippines, US SOF is working by, through, and with the Philippine military and executing strategies parallel to Dhofar's but implementing differently. However, in Afghanistan, the successful hearts and minds methods previously applied in other conflicts is falling short of expectations.

---

[1]Gian Gentile, "A Strategy of Tactics: Population Centric COIN and the Army," *Parameters* (Autumn 2009): 5-17.

[2]Department of the Army, Field Manual (FM) 3-24, *Counterinsurgency* (Washington, DC: Department of the Army, 2006), A-5.

CHAPTER 3

RESEARCH METHODOLOGY

Method

This thesis uses historical analysis, comparative case studies, and oral history interviews provided by counterinsurgency veterans from World War II (WWII) to recently returned practitioners from the Iraq, and Afghanistan conflict. The intent is two-fold. First, is to synthesize collected information in order to attain a definitive understanding of the hearts and minds concept. Second, explore its merit as a component of counterinsurgency campaigns. Although a significant number of oral history respondents are from the US and British militaries, several were from civilian think-tank organizations, interagency sectors, and national policy making institutions.

Interestingly, during the course of conducting oral history interviews for this paper, a noticeable difference in demeanor when hearts and minds are referenced by Americans and British participants. Americans were uncertain, to a point uncomfortable with the topic. When discussing the topic several felt they needed to explain their personal views in order to clarify the contextual angle they are approaching hearts and minds. Conversely, British participants exhibited a comfortable and seemingly clear grasp of the coercive history of heart and minds. Possibly the American participants' demeanor is closely related to their defeat in Vietnam. It remains as a significant emotional event in US history that undermines the effective understanding of hearts and minds. Alternatively, the British participants' seemingly comfortable demeanor could be attributed to their vast colonial past. They possessed a better understanding of hearts and minds concept, effectively employed it, and pioneered its application. According to Dr

Daniel Marston, "The history of British experience in creating, as well as living, fighting, and dying with indigenous forces, is generally considered one of the British Army's hallmark of excellence."[1] The British vast counterinsurgency experience can be traced from early colonial conflicts of the 19th century to the Second Anglo-Boer War; from the Aid-to-the Civil Power in the Empire, Malayan Emergency, Dhofar Rebellion to the streets of Belfast and Londonderry.[2]

The four case studies included are the British efforts during the Malayan Emergency against predominantly Chinese insurgents from 1948 to 1960, British SOF counterinsurgency efforts in Dhofar from 1970 to 1975, current US SOF efforts in support of the Philippine military against Islamic extremists in Mindanao, and the ongoing US-led ISAF efforts in Afghanistan. This work will examine the history behind the controversy surrounding the hearts and minds concepts and its current applications hits and misses.

Rationale for Case Studies Selected

The case studies were selected because each adds certain insights into a counterinsurgent force's application of hearts and minds. The four case studies are divided into two historical and two contemporary. The British successful prosecution of the Malayan Emergency against a communist insurgency is significant since heart and minds was coined by Gerald Templer during conflict. Conversely, the British highly coercive methods are a source of disagreement in interpretation. On the contrary, a decade later a much smaller contingent of British SOF in Dhofar similarly achieved victory against another communist insurgency with minimal application of coercion. The British worked through the prism of the Oman government and aided the host

24

government in winning its population's heart and minds. The fact that both British efforts delivered victory even with a diametric blend of coercion and persuasion is worth examining and could potentially be replicated today.

The ongoing US SOF effort in the southern Philippines merits inclusion among the case studies for several reasons. First, unbeknownst to many, the US achieved not one but three historical counterinsurgency victories in the Philippines: the Phil-American War (1899 to 1902), the Moro Rebellion (1902 to 1913), and the first victory over communism in Asia by assisting the Philippine government defeat the communist Hukbalahap (1946 to 1954). Second, US SOF lines of operation parallel those applied by British SAS in Dhofar but with a different implementation. Third, it portrays how a small but specialized force can assist indigenous forces win its population's heart and minds. Fourth, efforts in the southern Philippines are achieving considerable progress, why is this happening?

Lastly, this paper will be in remiss if Afghanistan is not included as a case study. It is America's longest and continuing conflict in history. An examination of the US-led ISAF hearts and minds efforts in Afghanistan in comparison to the other three case studies provides a point of reflection for current operations. This may show merits or perhaps deny or confirm the benefits of applying methods previously tried in history.

Limitations

In general, this thesis operates under two limitations. First, since the US is still actively prosecuting the conflicts in the southern Philippines and Afghanistan, it will not venture into classified information. In order to be of utility to the military reader, it will only examine operations from unclassified sources. Doing so would preclude its widest dissemination. Secondly, the four case studies do not provide an analysis of all the counterinsurgency methods applied or efforts by interagency organizations. In particular, U.S. Agency for International Development (USAID) has a significant role in development and legitimacy both of which are leveraged for winning hearts and minds. This thesis will remain in the bounds of military activities and actors; limit itself to hearts and minds methods.

Key Terms

In order to gain a better grasp of heart and minds, it is necessary to establish a common definition of the following terms: counterinsurgency, grievance, human rights, insurgency, legitimacy, and modernization theory.

Counterinsurgency: US joint doctrine defines counterinsurgency as, "military, paramilitary, political, economic, psychological, and civic actions taken by a government to defeat insurgency."[3] The word in itself depicts a reactionary nature to an insurgency. History is replete with incidents of governments' initial surprise, ambivalence, or incoherent initial response to an insurgency.[4] Much too often, governments fail to immediately identify the onset of an insurgency and when they do, governments counters with a conventional strategy based on attrition. Consequently, governments are embroiled in a protracted conflict of attrition that further alienates the population. It fails to realize that the people are the insurgents' source of resources, recruits, freedom of movement, and safe havens. According to Mao, who arguably is one of the most prolific and successful insurgency practitioners, "Weapons are an important factor in war, but not the decisive one; it is man and not the material that counts."[5] He preached that, "The guerrilla must move amongst the people as a fish swims in the sea."[6] Accordingly, an insurgency's

26

physical and psychological access of the population must be severed for counterinsurgent forces to win. Governments must not only defeat the insurgent's attempts to mobilize the people, but must mobilize the people themselves. To limit themselves to any effort less than their adversaries will be to invite failure.[7]

It is a battle for the population's hearts and minds. The protection and control of the population are emphasized by numerous classical counterinsurgency strategist and practitioners. Foremost is David Galula who asserted is his first law of counterinsurgency, "The support of the population is as necessary for the counterinsurgents as for the insurgents."[8] Robert Thompson reinforces Galula's assertion with, "An insurgent movement is a war for the people" and continues with, "The government must give priority to defeating the political subversion not the guerillas."[9] Taking all these in consideration, this paper defines counterinsurgency as - efforts taken by an established government to defeat an armed segment of the population whose aim is to reach its goals outside confines of established laws; successful counterinsurgency operation must provide security for and gain its population's heart and minds.

Grievance: Time and again an insurgency is given rise by a grievance emanating from a segment of the society that is willing to take arms. This grievance is transformed to a meaningful and appealing narrative[10] or a cause to take arms against a ruling establishment. When a government fails to address these grievances, often due to indifference or it is unworkable within the framework of the law, the discontented group organizes and initiates violence, which typically evolves into a protracted struggle against the government. Historical insurgent causes could be for sovereignty from colonial masters as fought by the Filipinos against Spain and the US in the early 1900s; political

27

equality for immigrant races as demanded by the Malayan Races Liberation Army (MRLA); or could be tied to land reform as demanded by the Hukbalahap in the Philippines immediately following WWII; or a call for social justice as in the case of Dhofar Liberation Front (DLF) in Oman; or regional autonomy for ethnic minorities seen in Dhofar and currently being waged by the Muslim Moros in the southern Philippines for almost five centuries. At the same time, all local seeds of conflict within a community can be exploited, as between young and old, between progressive and traditional, between different foreign capitalists. There is always some issue which has an appeal to each section of the society, and, even if dormant, an incident may easily revive it in an acute form.[11]

Human Rights: Rights inherent to all human beings, whatever nationality, place of residence, sex, national or ethnic origin, color, religion, language, or any other status. Universal human rights are often expressed and guaranteed by law, in the forms of treaties, customary international law, general principles and other sources of international law. International human rights law lays down obligations of governments to act in certain ways to refrain from certain acts, in order to promote and protect human rights and fundamental freedoms of individuals or groups.[12]

Insurgency: US joint doctrine defines insurgency as, "an organized movement aimed at the overthrow of a constituted government through the use of subversion and armed conflict."[13] However, an insurgency is not always after the overthrow of the government or for the imposition of an alternate regime but could be for a limited objective as in the case of the Dhofaris in Oman or the Moros in Mindanao. To this, Kitson offers a more encompassing purpose to insurgency, "the ultimate aim of an

28

insurgent organization is to overthrow a government or force it to do something it does not want to do."[14] While Mark O'Neill is of the same thought, "an organized, violent and politically motivated activity conducted by non-state actors and sustained over a protracted period that typically utilizes a number of methods, such as subversion, guerilla warfare and terrorism, in an attempt to achieve change within a state."[15] The ultimate aim of an insurgent organization is to force a government to do something it does not want to do and it needs to get the backing of a proportion of the population.

The population's support, or at a minimum its passive tolerance is required for an insurgent organization to thrive for it is militarily inferior at its inception. Sir Frank Kitson states, "It (insurgency) will first have to get the backing of a proportion of the population, if it is to stay in being and to fight: insurgents are bound to rely to a considerable extent on the people for money, shelter, food, and information."[16] It seeks refuge within the human terrain by blending in. The population is not only providing the guerilla with food and intelligence, but giving him perfect cover and concealment. Dressed as a peasant, the guerilla, except when he is carrying arms, is indistinguishable from the rest of the people. He is a peasant by day and a guerilla by night.[17] This paper defines insurgency as - an organized armed resistance with a protracted based politico-military strategy designed to remove or weaken the control and legitimacy of an established government, occupying power, or other political authority in order to impose its will.

Legitimacy: It is based on the legality, morality, and rightness of the actions undertaken.[18] The primary objective of any counterinsurgency operation is to foster development of effective governance by a legitimate government.[19] In Western liberal tradition, a government that derives its just powers from the people and responds to their desires while looking out for their welfare is accepted as legitimate. In contrast, theocratic societies fuse political and religious authority; political figures are accepted as legitimate because the populace views them as implementing the will of God.[20]

Modernization Theory: The theory is based on the purposeful development of societies through several stages of modernization from primitive traditional forms toward Western-style industrialization, secularization, and political pluralism.[21] It looks at the internal factors of a country while assuming that, with assistance, "traditional" countries can be brought to development in the same manner more developed Western countries have. It attempts to identify the social variables which contribute to social progress and development of societies, and seeks to explain the process of social evolution. The theory not only stresses the process of change but also the responses to that change, and also looks at internal dynamics while referring to social and cultural structures and the adaptation of new technologies.

---

[1]Daniel Marston, "Adaptation in the Field: The British Army's Difficult Campaign in Iraq," *Security Challenges* 6, no. 1 (Autumn 2010), 72.

[2]But on the contrary, Dr Marston argues that the British military failed to leverage its vast counterinsurgency experience as evident by its performance in Iraq.

[3]Department of Defense, Joint Publication (JP) 1-02, *Department of Defense Dictionary of Military and Associated Terms* (Washington, DC: Department of Defense, 2010).

[4]This was evident in Irish War of Independence (1919-1921), Malayan Emergency (1948-1960), Algerian War (1954-1962), Vietnam War (1955-1975), Dhofar Rebellion (1962-1975), Iraq War (2003), and Afghanistan War (2001).

[5]Mao Tse-Tung, *Selected Works, Vol. II*, 192. Worthy of note, Mao contradicted himself with, "Political power grows out of the barrel of a gun." Ibid. 272.

[6]Mao Tse-Tung, *On Guerrilla Warfare* (New York: Dover Publications, 2005), 41.

[7]John McCuen, *The Art of Counter-Revolutionary War* (Harrisburg, PA: Stockpole Books, 1966), 56.

[8]David Galula, *Counterinsurgency Warfare: Theory and Practice* (London: Pall Mall Press, 1964), 74.

[9]Ibid., 88.

[10]Narrative is the central mechanism, expressed in story form, through which ideologies are expressed and absorbed. Department of the Army, FM 3-24, 366.

[11]Robert Thompson, *Defeating Communist Insurgency* (London: Chatto and Windus, 1966), 21.

[12]United Nations Office of the High Commissioner for Human Rights (OHCHR), http://www.ohchr.org/EN/Issues/Pages/WhatareHumanRights.aspx (accessed 15 November 2010).

[13]Department of Defense, JP 1-02

[14]Command and General Staff College (CGSC) Scholars Program 2010, *CGSC Scholars Program Counterinsurgency Research Study 2010* (Fort Leavenworth, KS: Ike Skelton Chair in Counterinsurgency, 2010), AA1009.

[15]Mark O'Neill, *Confronting the Hydra* (Sydney: Lowy Institute, 2009), 7.

[16]Frank Kitson, *Bunch of Five* (London: Faber and Faber, 1977), 282.

[17]Thompson, *Defeating Communist Insurgency*, 34.

[18]Joint Chief of Staff, Joint Publication (JP) 3-0, *Joint Operations* (Washington, DC: Government Printing Office, 2008), A-4.

[19]Department of the Army, Field Manual 3-24, 37-39.

[20]Ibid.

[21]Michael Fitzsimmons, "Hard Hearts and Open Minds? Governance, Identity and the Intellectual Foundations of Counterinsurgency Strategy." *Journal of Strategic Studies* 31 (June 2008): 342-347.

CHAPTER 4

FOUR CASE STUDIES: MALAYA, DHOFAR, PHILIPPINES, AFGHANISTAN

Malaya[1]

The answer lies not in pouring more troops into the jungle, but in the heart and minds of the Malayan People.[2]

— Field Marshal Sir Gerald Walter Robert Templer

DUE TO COPYRIGHT RESTRICTIONS
SOME OR ALL IMAGES ARE NOT INCLUDED

Figure 1.   Map of Malaya
Source: Psywar.org, http://www.psywar.org/malaya.php (accessed 4 January 2011).

The British/Malayan prosecution of the Malayan Emergency (1948 to 1960)

following World War II is considered a classic counterinsurgency model. The

British/Malayan victory demonstrated how a communist insurgency could be defeated in a predominantly Muslim nation by Western-led forces. Its success is arguably a model

against which other classical counterinsurgency campaigns are measured. The

Emergency was discussed heavily within US circles as possible model for tactics

techniques and procedures for the Vietnam War. Gerard Templer introduced the term

hearts and minds in Malaya, something generally associated with a less coercive

approach to counterinsurgency which emphasizes the importance of using minimum

force in order to win the hearts and minds of the people. However, the methods applied in

Malaya do not adhere to this definition. The British counterinsurgency campaigns

involved a considerable degree of coercion and even abuse of human rights if measured

in today's standards.[3]

World War II left the Malayan economy disrupted and ailing from high

unemployment, low wages, and scarce and expensive food. The British administration

with its own devastated home economy was attempting to repair Malaya's economy

quickly, especially as revenue from Malaya's tin and rubber industries was important to

Britain's own post-war recovery. As a result, protesters were dealt with harshly, by

measures including arrests and deportations. The Malayan Communist National Party

(MCP) with its armed wing, the Malayan National Liberation Army (MNLA),[4] succeeded

in gaining control over the trade union organization, and used its influence to advance its

political agenda to destabilize the British administration in Malaya.[5] Their ultimate

objective was clear - to gain independence from British colonization and establish a

communist government. The MCP/MNLA was dominated by a Chinese minority who

were oppressed, denied voting and land ownership rights, and impoverished. The

insurgent's support base was internal and came from an ethnic Chinese minority group,

33

the Min Yuen. This was the spy network for the MCP; its role was to channel intelligence, supplies, and new recruits to the units in the jungles and to engage in espionage and assassinations. The MRLA relied on Min Yuen for food, money, information, and dissemination of their propaganda.[6]

On 16 June 1948, MNLA committed its first overt act of the war when three European plantation managers were killed at Sungai Siput, Perak. This forced the Commonwealth's declaration of the Emergency.[7] Harsh Emergency Regulations were enacted that included the death penalty for the offense of carrying arms, the suspension of the writ of habeas corpus, searches without warrants authorities could impose curfews and control the movement of persons and vehicles.[8] The British administration basically changed the law in order to legitimize coercive methods that would halt the deterioration of civil order. The initial campaign plan was designed in two parts. First, security forces initially took defensive action by providing guards to vital key points such as power stations, police stations, public utilities, and tin mines, with the objective to protect them from MCP sabotage action. Second, security forces, with the participation of the Commonwealth troops, would conduct major military operations, against the MRLA aimed at neutralizing insurgents in the jungle. These operations involved the destruction of the insurgents' camps, cutting off their food supply, and the uncovering dumps of arms and equipment.[9]

It soon became evident that neither the British administration nor the insurgents were prepared for this conflict. Both sides were tactically groping their way in the dark. When the MNLA launched its first guerilla operations and forced the Emergency declaration, the British response was typical of most governments' initial reaction to an insurgency it was surprised and responded with a strategy centered on enemy kill-capture

using large conventional forces and static security on economic targets. Soldier and

author Richard Clutterbuck captures the British soldiers' mindset at that time:

> The predilection of some army officers for major operations seems incurable.
> Even in the late 1950's, new brigade commanders would arrive from England,
> nostalgic for World War II, or fresh from large-scale maneuvers in Germany. On
> arrival in Malaya, they would address themselves with chinagraphs to a map
> almost wholly green except for one red pin. "Easy," they would say. "Battalion on
> the left, battalion on the right, battalion blocking the end, and then a fourth
> battalion to drive through. Can't miss, old boy." Since it took the better part of a
> day, with more than a thousand soldiers, to get an effective cordon even a half-
> mile square around a jungle camp, the guerrillas, hearing the soldiers crashing
> through the jungle into position, had no difficulty getting clear before the net was
> closed. Except for a rare brush with a straggler, all the soldiers ever found was an
> empty camp, but this enabled the officers to claim they had "cleared the area of
> enemy." This would be duly marked on the maps, and the commanders would go
> to bed with a glow of satisfaction over a job well done. The soldiers, nursing their
> blisters, had other words for it.[10]

On the other hand, the MCP/MRLA was ill-equipped and lacked a coherent plan

during the initial stage of the campaign that saved the British administration from a quick

defeat. The British action against the Trade Union Organization, the disbanding of the

MCP as a legal organization, and the introduction of the Emergency Regulation had taken

the MCP by surprise.[11] A better equipped and more properly planned guerrilla campaign

by the MRLA could have brought the Malayan economy to the brink of disaster.[12]

The initial counterinsurgency effort of 1948 to 1950 proved inadequate, confused,

and undermanaged.[13] General Sir Harold Briggs was brought in to turn the tide and

appointed British Army Director of Operations.[14] He implemented a multifaceted

counterinsurgency strategy that became known as the Briggs Plan. He believed that to

win the war against the communist guerrillas, the British administration would need to

gain the support from the Chinese, because the majority of the MCP members were

Chinese. He understood that the guerilla's tactics relied on the Chinese masses and that in order to end the insurgency the government forces have to protect and control the population by isolating them from the guerrillas.[15] His successor General Sir Gerald Templer continued and improved this plan.

Throughout the counterinsurgency campaign, effective small unit kinetic operations continued aimed at neutralizing those deemed irreconcilables. Military operations continued in concert with the rest of the British strategy which included four other lines of efforts: good governance, interagency coordination, capacity building of indigenous forces, and population and resource control. The British promoted governance by continuing to build the ability of the Malayan people to govern themselves in preparation for the promised independence. On 31 August 1957 the British government delivered on that promise. By assuring and granting Malayan independence, the British addressed a primary MCP/MNLA grievance and effectively eliminating it from the insurgent's narrative--the removal of colonial rule, as well as inclusion of the Chinese community within the future Malayan political apparatus and process. The insurgent had a cause that the counterinsurgent espoused without unduly endangering its power. The counterinsurgent had to promise the necessary reforms, and then implement them, which they did.[16] Effectively, the Commonwealth pulled the rug from under the insurgents. Sovereignty was primary major grievance, the foundation of their cause and the British took the revolution from the revolutionaries.

Interagency coordination or unity of effort could be categorized as a second line of effort. Templer was direct on his intent, "Any idea that the business of normal civil government and the business of the Emergency are two separate entities must be killed for good and for all. The two activities are completely and utterly interrelated."[17] The

highest direction and operational conduct of counterinsurgency throughout the 1948-1960

Malayan Emergency was on both a joint civil-military and a combined British-Malayan

basis.[18] Briggs introduced the War Executive Committees at federal, state and district

level, this improved planning and cooperation drastically especially between civil, police

and military.[19] It provided a viable managerial device for integrating British and Malayan

efforts and for pulling together the multiple strands of counterinsurgency operations.

Enabling an indigenous government to fight its own war is a key to a unified

counterinsurgency policy.

A third line of effort was building the capacity of indigenous security forces by

increasing their size, capability, and delegating the role of intelligence gathering to the

police. The term police is interpreted here as paramilitary police force or local security

forces recruited from the same community, the Home Guard. They belong to the same

ethnicity as the people they are tasked to secure and protect. The security forces were

equipped with new weapons and armored vehicles to conduct the military operations

against the MCP militant wings and the police underwent the special training on criminal

investigation and intelligence collections. In addition, the male population was

encouraged to join the Home Guards to protect their villages throughout the country and

to help the police to maintain security.[20]

Effective counterinsurgency relies on good human intelligence, and no military

unit can match a good police unit in developing an accurate human intelligence picture of

their area of operations.[21] This was evident in the build-up of the Special Branch (SB)

and the Senoi Pra'aq (fighting aborigines). Since Malayan Emergency was classified as civil unrest, the intelligence role was given to the police. The police SB had the sensitive task of maintaining situational awareness of subversive groups. Their activities during the Emergency were widely praised. It was during this period that the British "Malaysianized" the Special Branch by replacing its crop of British spies and officers with trained locals, including Chinese.[22] The reason was simple, the SB officers, staffs, and agents live in the local area, speak the language and know the people. They are of the people. Their ability cannot be replicated by even the best trained foreign troops and not even by army intelligence staffs who are continually rotating.[23]

The Senoi Pra'aq (fighting aborigines) was formed to expand local security forces in the insurgents' sanctuaries. They were trained by the British Army's 22 Special Air Service (SAS) Regiment and administered by the Department of Aborigines.[24] This strike force of about three hundred was highly effective and credited with killing more guerillas than the rest of the security forces put together during the final two years of the conflict.

In addition, Templer continued the tactical innovations from the Briggs Plan and turned it into doctrine. He ordered the creation of a manual that would "encapsulate the wealth of jungle fighting experience in such a way as to fit in the pocket of a soldier's jungle greens." The Anti-Terrorism Operations in Malaya (ATOM) manual became the bible of British counterinsurgency. It was written by the same Lieutenant Colonel Walter Walker who had created Far East Land Force (FARELF) Training Center (FTC)[25] and the Ferret Force. Templer also established an operations research training center to collate information on the progress of the COIN effort and to focus all efforts on the collection of intelligence on the abilities.[26]

Lastly, but most significantly, a forceful population and resource control method was vigorously employed that was synonymous to a carrot-and-stick (reward and punishment) policy. The "stick" portion was a huge undertaking. More than half a million people, of whom 400,000 were Chinese, were resettled from their dwellings located at edges of the jungle and into government regulated "New Villages." These new communes were subjected to pervasive food controls and food-denial operations, surrounded by fences and police posts. Access to each New Village was tightly controlled. Residents were subjected to search upon exit and entry. Smuggling food, medicine, or other militarily useful items was subject to severe punishment.[27] The strategy was based on "draining the swamp" approach. By denying the insurgents' access to the population, they are effectively severed from their source of food, supplies and manpower.

As for the other side of the carrot-and-stick strategy, when Templer took over from Briggs, he continued and enhanced the Briggs Plan by implementing an effective hearts and minds campaign to better the living conditions of the Chinese squatters. The New Villages afforded the settlers protection and made them less prone to insurgent intimidations.[28] Providing a sense of security, comfort and safety are important aspects in winning hearts and minds. A massive development and modernization effort was launched in order to upgrade the standard of living of the people. Templer granted Malay citizenship en masse to over a million Chinese (a major grievance) and Indians; required Britons to register as Malay citizens; elevated the public role of women; constructed schools clinics, and police stations; electrified rural villages; continued a 700 percent increase in the number of police and military troops; and gave arms to militia guards to protect their own communities.[29] Rather than spending a disproportionate effort finding

and killing the insurgents it was more effective and economical to deprive the insurgents

of those essentials on which they depend to survive namely the support of the local

population, bases, mobility, supplies and information, although military operations

continued.[30]

Eventually, the coercive methods coupled with providing basic needs as water and

electricity, new roads, school, and medical assistance in the New Villages produced the

desired behavior. By implementing the hearts and minds approach, the population began

to appreciate the improved living conditions in the resettlements compared to their

original communities and began to sever ties with the insurgents. By early 1953,

Templer's enhanced Briggs Plan had significantly impacted the MCP militant subversive

activities and breaking the back of the insurgency in about five years.[31]

A significant "carrot" is lifting the Emergency regulations (restrictions) once an

area is declared "white" or deemed clear of insurgents. On 28 August 1953, Malacca was

declared the first white area in Malaya.[32] The Emergency regulations were relaxed,

curfews were lifted, and food controls lifted.[33] When the first general election was held in

Malaya in 1955, Tunku Abdul Rahman was elected as the first Chief Minister of the

Federation of Malaya. This was a major political success as Malays were now given the

opportunity to govern themselves, leading to eventual independence from Great British.

Tunku then declared an amnesty for all the MCP's guerillas. This led to the MCP

leadership decision to negotiate with the Malayan Government to end the insurgency.

The meeting was held in Baling, Kedah (Northern Malaya) in December 1955 (known as

The Baling Talks). The MCP agreed to end their armed struggle if the Malayan

Government recognized the Communist Party of Malaya as a legal political party, allowing them to take part in the independence process. Tunku refused to accept the condition and the meeting ended as a failure for both sides. Political legitimacy had failed for the MCP and the government failed to end the insurgency prior to its independence on 31 August 1957. This had a devastating effect on MCP propaganda, which had focused on gaining independence from the British through communist success. Subsequently, the MCP lost significant support from the Chinese population. After independence in 1957, the British began to allow the Malayan government handle security matters. On 31 July 1960, the Malaya Government declared the end of the Emergency in Malaya, although the war against the communist insurgency never really ended, until the 1980s. The declaration only ended the usage of Emergency laws.[34] However, this set the conditions for the Second Malaysian Emergency that reignited in 1968 but ended with victory for the now independent Malaysian government in 1989.

Malaya's Legacy

The successful British counterinsurgency campaign during the Malayan Emergency has and will always be plundered for lessons learned and looked upon as an example. Unfortunately, it left a historical hole of ambiguity. The question that begs to be answered is, "Was the Malayan Emergency strategy one of hearts and minds?" Templer's proclaimed hearts and minds campaign in Malaya may serve to conceal the extent to which the British used coercion and repression. It left an open door for debate. On one side, are those who argue that success in Malaya was due to the hearts and minds counterinsurgency approach, even if it involved high levels of force and coercion. On the other side are those who argue that the highly oppressive measure rendered hearts and minds insignificant. As British Colonel David Benest argues, "Bluntly put, coercion was the reality–'hearts and minds' a myth."[35] Lieutenant Colonel Wade Markel, a US Army strategist who has served in Afghanistan, is of the same conclusion. He states that it was the British "strategy of population control" and other repressive measures (rather than hearts and minds) which were successful in Malaya. Markel's conclusion from his comparative analysis of Malaya, Kenya and Vietnam is that the vital element in both (Malaya and Kenya) counterinsurgency efforts was the effective internment of the subject populations, and not efforts at social amelioration. While we would like to believe that winning hearts and minds is both important and effective, these examples suggest that the effort is neither essential nor decisive.[36]

Although several policies were enacted to improve the lot of the squatter Chinese population, the campaign was dominated by severely coercive and intrusive methods such as: resettlement, food denial, mass arrests and punishment, the death penalty for carrying arms, detention without trial, deportations, identity cards and movement restriction, collective punishment in the form of curfews and fines, and hanging hundreds of prisoners.[37] Hearts and minds conceals the reality that the counterinsurgency campaign involved high levels of coercion and draconian methods in today's standards. However, all were conducted within the revised law as skillfully accommodated in the Emergency regulations. The coercion deployed by the British in Malaya was not an isolated case, in Kenya the British campaign against the Mau-Mau was also conducted with considerable force and brutality.[38]

Perhaps the draconian methods in Malaya escaped media scrutiny. In the era of globalization, by contrast, where transnational connectivity ensured that ideas, capital, goods, services, and information can be transferred in near real time across borders, there would be no lack of media intrusion.[39] Today's highly advanced broadcast technology capable of 24-hour news coverage, instantaneous broadcast, and empowered individuals by cell phone cameras and internet connectivity, the highly coercive methods seen in Malaya could backfire and ignite global condemnation. You can no longer forcefully relocate half-a-million civilians in New Villages, burn their old dwellings, deny food and water to villages suspected of aiding insurgents, mass detain without trials, or shoot people for breaking curfews. Other than erecting T-wall barriers to separate communities, conducting cordon and searches, and imposing curfews, methods seen in Malaya simply cannot be applied today without exposure to strategic failure.

A second point that contributed to the British administration's resettlement success was that the Chinese squatters were not rooted to the land. They were mostly squatters and foreigners. Consider this method in a different setting where the population is tied to ancestral or tribal lands, the same strategy would be met with greater resistance and such was the case in Vietnam with the failed Strategic Hamlet Program. The mostly-Buddhist peasantry practiced ancestor worship, an important part of their religion that was disrupted by being forced out of their villages and away from their ancestors' graves. Some who resisted the resettlement were summarily executed by government forces conversely increasing population support for the insurgents.[40] Current case-in-points are the Moros in the southern Philippines fighting for ancestral domain and the Taliban's contention against continued coalition forces (infidels) presence by in Muslim territory.

Another British advantage in Malaya was their colonial presence. It allowed some familiarity with the culture, terrain, language, and peoples, however, they had to learn quickly when it came to the Chinese population. US forces face this challenge in current counterinsurgency campaigns (e.g. Iraq and Afghanistan). It is extremely difficult to harness the maximum potential of a hearts and minds strategy if you are a foreigner dealing with an unfamiliar culture, history, and with no strand of familiarity to the people you are trying to influence. In addition, as colonial masters of Malaya the British had the power to grant independence. By promising independence and fulfilling this promise, they took an important aspect of the MCP's narrative.

Finally, Dixon argues that the definition of hearts and minds is associated with different attitudes to the role of human rights and the level of force that it is appropriate to deploy in a counterinsurgency. Those wishing to win the consent and support of the population may well use less violence and coercion, with a higher regard for human rights because they believe that is more likely to win the positive endorsement of the people and this is necessary if the objective is to establish a democracy. Those who wish merely to win the acquiescence, "respect," toleration or fear of the population may believe that this is possible even with the use of much higher levels of violence and that this had been the recipe for success in the British Empire.[41] Undoubtedly, the application of coercive methods of separating the population from the insurgents played a critical role in the British success. The massive control and intimidation, with the key to the campaign relying more in "screwing down the people" than in winning their hearts and minds; "the back of the Emergency was broken by a 'law and order' and resettlement approach, with 'hearts and minds' tactics playing an important but auxiliary role."[42] The debate will continue for generations to come in reference to hearts and minds in Malaya but in today's context those coercive methods will be difficult to replicate.

Do not try to do too much with your own hands. Better the Arabs do it tolerably than that you do it perfectly. It is their war, and you are to help them, not to win it for them.[44]

— Lieutenant Colonel Thomas Edward Lawrence

Winning a counterrevolutionary war is like clearing a garden of weeds, it is what you plant afterwards that matters.[45]

— Major General Tony Jeapes

Figure 2.   Map of Oman

Source: Central Intelligence Agency, The World Factbook, Oman, https://www.cia.gov/library/publications/theworld-factbook/ geos/mu.html (accessed 1 November 2010).

Eclipsed by the Vietnam War, Cold War in Europe, and later by the 'Troubles' in Northern Ireland, the Dhofar Rebellion was a successful counterinsurgency campaign. It was a war won by the host nation, Oman, and intervening foreign forces, British, through the application hearts and minds methods on top of excellent military strategy and tactics.[46] The British Special Air Services (SAS) and the Omani government waged an effective counterinsurgency campaign against communist insurgents. The Dhofar Rebellion is a model for SOF foreign intervention.

It offers unique insights into one of the few instances where an Islamic state, backed by a small number of Western SOF, defeated a Marxist insurgency during the Cold War.[47] Unlike the Malayan Emergency campaign that was primarily conducted and led by conventional forces, the Dhofar Rebellion was supported by a small number of British SAS who worked within the sovereign authority of Sultanate of Oman and the Sultan's Armed Forces (SAF).[48] Author and retired SAS Paul Sibley comments on the chief missions of the SAS:

> We had two objectives. One was to raise Firqats. These were groups of surrendered enemy personnel (SEPs). Essentially they were Jebel tribesmen who had changed sides and wanted to fight for the Sultan. The function of the BATT (British Army Training Teams) was to raise them with heavy weapon support, and gain information from them. The first firqat, the Firqat Salahadin was multi-tribal. There was much quarrelling, and subsequent firqats were based on single tribes. Our other aim was to provide local assistance to the civilian population as CATs (Civil Action Teams). This took many forms, running clinics, supplying fresh water, food, veterinary assistance, tents, etc.[49]

Besides the British contribution of SAS and seconded and contracted British officers, equally significant, especially in the realm of propaganda, was the support by an Iranian battle group and Jordanian SOF and engineer battalion.

The insurgency that faced the Sultanate in 1962 was centered in the southwestern province of Dhofar, located over 500 miles from the capital in Muscat. The northern part of the province encompasses the final 400 miles of the vast Arabian Desert, the "empty quarter." Between the desert and the sea lies the two Jebel, rugged mountain ranges that parallel the coast to the border with South Yemen. In some places the mountains reach 5,000 feet, the entire area pockmarked with caves, gullies and other obstacles that severely restrict any cross-country movement. Finally, there is a coastal strip, heavily vegetated and offering some suitable land for habitation.[50]

At its worst moment, government control in Dhofar was limited to a small area around Salalah on the coast. The airfield was being regularly mortared and there was a danger that the war would spread into the rest of Oman. If this had happened, Western access to the Gulf oil would have been seriously jeopardized and it was therefore vitally important that Oman should not fall under communist rule. It is a rarity in a counterinsurgency campaign to pinpoint one critical event that turned a conflict around. For the Dhofar Rebellion, Sultan Qaboos' ascension as the Sultanate of Oman on 23 July 1970 was that moment. Prior to that, the communist insurgency was well on its way to victory, but Qaboos' successful coup d'état against his father Sultan bin Taimur, empowered him to unify command and effort. The communist insurgency was defeated within the next six years.

The policies imposed by Qaboos' father, Sultan bin Taimur, in Dhofar, or the lack thereof, created the discontent that fueled rebellion. The insurgent Dhofar Liberation Front (DLF), that was later dominated and taken over by the Popular Front for the Liberation of Occupied Arabian Gulf (PFLOAG), was born out of oppressive government policies. The DLF initiated guerilla operations in 1962 against the Sultanate of Muscat and Oman. The DLF's primary grievance was based on their ethnicity's marginalization and neglect. The Sultan bin Taimur had kept the country firmly in the middle ages by his feudal system of government and his refusal to allow any kind of modernization.[51] In

47

1965, there was only one primary school and no medical facilities in the province. There was no electricity or running water. Only one road, unpaved, connected the province with the rest of the nation.[52] Omanis in general, and Dhofaris in particular, were not allowed to possess radios, play music, dance, smoke, wear Western clothes or take pictures; infractions were punishable by imprisonment or flogging. Communities that violated the Sultan's dictates were subject to collective punishments to include the cementing over of village wells and destruction of the walls protecting crops. Taxation policies were also extortionate, import taxes for Dhofar were 300 percent higher than the rest of the country, fishermen paid a daily tax on catches, and herders paid both monthly and annual taxes on their animals.[53] Some demanded social justice but Taimur's responded only with heavy-handed search and destroy missions that further alienated the Dhofar's population. Under Taimur's orders homes of suspected insurgents were burned and civilians from the Dhofar Jebel[54] were denied access to the markets in the towns on the plain where they traditionally sold their livestock. These measures virtually forced the uncommitted Dhofari population into the rebels' arms.[55] As one visiting economist noted:

> There was great poverty and disease . . . yet nothing was done because the Sultan would not permit it. No man could leave his village and seek work without the permission of the Sultan. No man could repair his house without the permission of the Sultan. This remote old man . . . had instilled such a fear in his people that very few of them dared defy him and undertake any initiative to improve their lot.[56]

The situation turned dire for Taimur's government when DLF joined forces with the PFLOAG. This was a partnership primarily based on the proverbial, "the enemy of my enemy is my friend." The PFLOAG was a communist organization with heavy backing from the Chinese and later from the Soviet consulates in Aden in the form of arms, money and training. The DLF were initially lukewarm about the PFLOAG but was finally seduced by the money and superior weapons PFLOAG could offer.[57] This

partnership of convenience would eventually crumble due to theological dichotomy. The

DLF was firmly grounded in Islam while PFLOAG espoused an atheist-communist creed.

Ultimately, the DLF was taken over by the more powerful PFLOAG. They used all the

traditional brutal Maoist techniques in the conflict, including breaking down the feudal

structures, killing the tribal and religious leaders and destroying the schools and mosques.

They created new party and militant groups which brutalized the local population.[58]

Taimur continued his oppressive strategy and after eight years of fighting with

victory nowhere in sight, his government had grown weaker and the insurgents stronger.

In Dhofar, control was limited to a small area around Salalah. His son, Qaboos bin Said,

committed the coup and immediately requested more British assistance. Concerned about

the prejudicial effects the insurgency could have on their decision to withdraw from the

Arabian Gulf in 1971 as well as the potential risk to the flow of oil through the Straits of

Hormuz, the Britain government decided to intervene,[59] Lieutenant Colonel John Watts,

Commander, 22nd SAS, deployed to Dhofar to assesses the situation. Based on

previously successful counterinsurgency operations in Malaya, he produced the blueprint

for support to the Sultan's government which became known as the Watts Plan. The Plan

was based on the method of combining military operations with a coordinated hearts and

minds campaign to win over the sympathy of the Dhofaris to the government cause:

1. Intelligence Operations- To clearly identify the enemy and friendly forces by establishing an effective intelligence collection and collation system;
2. Information Operations - To communicate clear intent to the insurgents, the population, and counter insurgent propaganda;
3. Medical Civic Action - To provide medical and dental aid to the people of Dhofaris, including those living in the Jebel;

4. Veterinary Civic Action - To provide veterinary services and fresh water for the cattle in the Dhofar region which are the main source of wealth
5. Capacity Building - To raise and train Dhofari soldiers, to fight for the Sultan.[60]

The number of SAS soldiers and support personnel eventually totaled to two SAS squadrons or about 500 men. Under Qaboos, with coalition support, the conflict began to turn in the governments favor. By January 1976 the war has been won by a combination good central/local government, oil money to modernize and equip the armed forces, and an effective joint civil-military strategy.

Oman's successful counterinsurgency operation was based on complementing and coordinated lines of efforts. It highlights the significance of amnesty, addressing an insurgency's primary grievance, unity of command, intelligence emphasis, sanctuary denial and sealing borders, and an effective hearts and minds approach. The success of the Dhofar counterinsurgency campaign can be attributed to several factors, foremost of which are the Oman government's efforts upon Sultan Qaboos' ascension to power. His unified command and social reform actions allowed him to establish legitimate governance in Dhofar. He immediately addressed the original grievance for social justice with a plan of action:

1. Offering a general amnesty to all those of his subjects who had opposed the Sultan.
2. Ending the archaic status of the Dhofar province and its incorporation in the state of Oman.
3. Opposing those insurgents who did not accept the general amnesty offer by conducting effective military operations, and
4. Improving the lives of the populace through a vigorous nation-wide development program.
5. A diplomatic initiative with two aims:
   a. Having Oman recognized as an Arab state with a legal form of government
   b. Isolating the PDRY from the support it was receiving from other Arab states.[61]

50

Sultan Qaboos moved quickly to address the critical issues of national development and to strengthen the SAF. To achieve these goals, he was able to draw upon the revenues derived from Oman's newly developed oil fields. With these funds, the Sultan was able to focus on developing Oman's infrastructure with a special emphasis on Dhofar. During the period of the counterinsurgency "some 40 per cent of government expenditures went to Dhofar . . . despite the fact that Dhofaris constituted only 10 per cent or so of the country's total citizenry."[62] Many of these expenditures went towards basic services in the Jebel to include wells, schools, mosques, roads and hospitals. In Salalah, the British opened a model experimental farm, conducted soil analysis for agricultural improvements, deployed veterinary teams and imported animals to help improve the native stock. All of these activities were directly supported by an aggressive psychological operations campaign aimed at winning the hearts and minds of the population. Qaboos' amnesty program, medical and veterinary civic action programs, and development initiatives earned him the confidence of formerly disenfranchised people and eroded the insurgent intellectual safe haven. By addressing the DLF's original grievance of social justice, human basic needs, and development, he took away a significant part of the PFLOAG's narrative.

Dhofar's Legacy

The overarching lesson of the Dhofar Rebellion for today's counterinsurgency practitioners is the nature of British SAS' excellent foreign intervention. Their task was to raise and train the Firqat tribesmen in cooperation with their attached units, all of which were known as British Army Training Team (BATT)(The British operations in

Oman were based around a hearts and minds campaign to win the people over from the Communist-backed Adoo guerrillas.

The British understood their role and despite the conflict's demand for a larger force, they declined and provided limited but sufficient resources. They knew that their stay was temporary, their efforts were only a stopgap, and that the final and enduring solution needed to come from the Omanis. By not sending a huge conventional force and committing only a small contingent of SAS operatives in the conflict, the Omanis were forced to build the force and solicit additional external support. By 1974 Iran had deployed a 1,200-man infantry battle group that included helicopter and logistical support, Jordan sent a SOF and an engineer battalion, and the United Kingdom provided seconded officers, helicopter support, and two SAS squadrons.[63] The arrival of Iranian and Jordanian forces distributed the hardship of combat and bolstered the legitimacy of the counterinsurgency campaigns with Muslim nations and the international community as a whole. This ended Oman's diplomatic isolation and facilitated entry into the United Nations and Arab League.[64]

The British forces worked by, through, and with the host nation and Sultan Qaboos maintained unity of command and the Omanis were on point. The hearts and minds effort was anchored on building the Sultan's legitimacy by addressing civil vulnerabilities. Ultimately, it is the host nation's security forces (army, police, and paramilitary) and institutions that sealed the victory against the insurgents and legitimized the rule of its government. Only local security forces can win their people's hearts and minds. This is one of the SAS most skillful achievements. Their support did not marginalize local security forces or erode the host nation government's legitimacy.

This is a stark contrast to US efforts in Iraq and Afghanistan; whereby, the continued presence of Western forces has delegitimized attempts in good governance and eroded the credibility the host nation's chief executives.

As advisors the BATTs held together the many disparate elements of the Sultan's forces , built the Firqats, and joined the Firqats in action against the Adoo.[65] The Firqats were surrendered enemy personnel (SEP). They spoke the dialect, understood the culture, and knew the terrain and the enemy since many were former Adoo. The Firqat owed its success to these skills and their capability cannot be replicated by any foreign troops. The British advisors might have the technical knowledge and know what needed to be said, but only local forces knew how to say it in such a way that it would appeal to the Dhofari mind.[66] Only the Dhofari mind could interpret for the Westerners how Dhofaris think.

After the Sultan of Oman Armed Forces (SAF), SAS and Firqats had established themselves on the Jebel, the Civil Action Teams (CAT) started to carry out hearts and minds operations that were anchored on limited modernization, essential services, and building the legitimacy of the new Sultan's government to win the support of the Dhofaris. The Dhofaris wanted good governance, which in their case did not include one man one vote, but infrastructure in the form of wells, roads, mosque, houses, and schools, and finally good veterinarians. Every successful military operation in the Jebel was immediately followed by the arrival of civil reconstruction teams.[67] The SAS went to great lengths to explain to the Dhofaris that they would be far better off to align themselves with the new Sultan rather than the communists.

Another hearts and minds aspect was the SAS support for Dhofari tribal traditions and respect for Islam. They did not impose a new political system and by respecting the

Arabs' devotion to Islam, SAS soldiers gained a lot of respect from the population; a significant aspect of Dhofari life that communists insurgents forbade. The SAS leveraged the religious divide between the insurgent and the populations through narratives anchored on, "Islam is prosperous with the Sultan, life is barren with the Communists" and "Freedom is our Aim, Islam is our way."[68]

Condition based hearts and minds approach is another legacy of this conflict. This is a significant lesson that most counterinsurgency practitioners miss. Without conditions, your hearts and minds efforts are hinged of wishful thinking or hopeful gratitude reciprocity. It is naïve to anticipate that people will reciprocate your goodwill and even if they initially do, all it takes is for the insurgents to intimidate the population and your efforts are wasted. Instead, use the humanitarian project as carrot with attached conditions. For instance, the SAS brought in British and Arab engineers with heavy drilling equipment to drill new water wells in the Jebel. After the SAF had occupied an area, the engineers would build wells, mosques and schools. The SAS then told the Dhofaris that if the Adoo returned to the area, they would cut the water off. An excellent example was provided by Brigadier John Akehurst, a commander in Dhofar:

> A SAF operation in strength supported by a Firqat secures a position of the Firqat's choice which dominated its tribal area. Military engineers build a track to the position giving road access, followed by an airstrip if possible. A drill is brought down the track followed by a Civil Action Team (who set up a) shop, school, clinic and mosque. SAF thins out to a minimum to provide security. Water is pumped to the surface and into distribution systems prepared by military engineers to offer storage points for humans and troughs for animals. Civilians come in from miles around to talk to the Firqat, SAF and government representatives. ***They are told that enemy activity in this area will result in the water being cut off.*** Civilians move out in surrounding areas and tell the enemy not to interfere with what is obviously a good thing (they also provided intelligence). Enemy, very dependent on the civilians, stops all aggressive action

and either goes elsewhere or hides. Tribal area is secure. All SAF are withdrawn. The SAS objective, codenamed.[69]

The formation of the irregular Firqat organization in 1971 subsequently allowed the development of vital knowledge and understanding of the Dhofar tribes. Without understanding the tribal dynamics and the aspiration of the Dhofaris, it would not have been possible to gain their support against the communists or develop an intelligence based strategy for the war.[70]

In Dhofar the British did not impose a different form of governance. They honored the existing social order and worked within the prevailing cultural and civil framework. The SAS tailored their operations in support of the host nation government's prism and legitimized Sultan Qaboos and his government by giving it credit for their work and placed an Omani face on the effort whenever possible. Somewhat similar to Malaya, the British had some presence in Oman providing them an edge in understanding the culture, language, and religion.

The Moro Islamic Liberation Front (MILF) describes the latest approach to the insurgency problem in Mindanao by the Armed Forces of the Philippines (AFP), which is civil-military operations, as more lethal than brute force.[72]

— Khaled Musa, Deputy Chairman,
Committee on Information, MILF

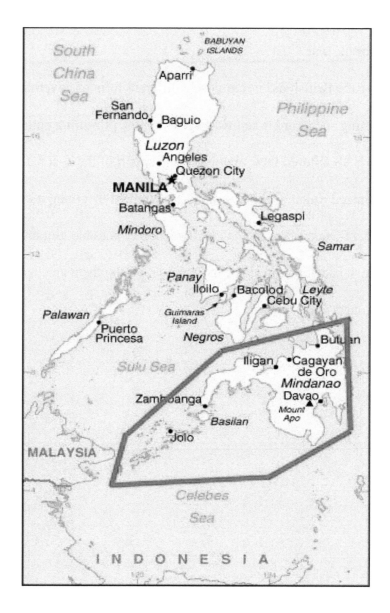

Figure 3. Map of the Philippines highlighting JSOTF-P Joint Operations Area
Source: Created by author. Central Intelligence Agency, The World Factbook, Philippines, https://www.cia.gov/library/publications/theworld-factbook/geos/rp.html (accessed 1 November 2010).

Commenting on the overall US counterinsurgency efforts, in his book *The Accidental Guerrilla*, David Kilcullen contends that the U.S. failure in understanding cultures has contributed to the creation of insurgents and guerillas. He argues that with a light footprint, the targeted use of military force, an increased focus on advisory role, and with a smarter use of economic support, we can conduct counterinsurgency using far less American resources while relying on local assets.[73] Evidently, the current US operations in the southern islands of the Republic of the Philippines (RP), fulfill Kilcullen's argument.[74]

The Joint Special Operations Forces Task Forces–Philippines (JSOTF-P) offers in many respects a commendable case study on how the evolved hearts and minds approach, one that is anchored on modernization and legitimacy with minimal coercion, is effectively employed and eroding popular support to insurgents. This is a counterinsurgency model worth examining. JSOTF-P's successes are grounded on conducting warfare "by, through, and with" surrogate forces. It is a proven method as executed by the British SAS in the Dhofar Rebellion (1970 to 1975).

Philippine relations remain vital to US defense and its fight against terrorism. The two countries shared history unveils a colonial past that afforded America not one, but three major successful counterinsurgency campaigns and a fourth currently being supported in the southern Philippines. This paper will be remiss not to briefly mention the Philippine-American War (1899 to 1902), Moro Rebellion (1902 to 1913) and the Hukbalahap Rebellion (1946 to 1954). However, the US military's institutional memory seems to have overlooked these successful counterinsurgency campaigns. FM 3-24, had only reference to the Philippine-American War, "The United States began the century by

57

defeating the Philippine Insurrection."[75] There was no mention of the successful

pacification of the Moros and the role US advisors played in defeating the Hukbalahap

(Huks). Both conflicts impart several salient themes in understanding the current

counterinsurgency campaigns raging in the southern Philippines. Unfortunately, the

successes in the last two counterinsurgency campaigns contributed to the current conflict

raging in Mindanao, the southern Philippines.[76] First, the US-Moro Bates Treaty kept the

Moros[77] neutral during the Philippine-American War against Filipino Christians.

However, the Treaty brought recognition to Moro sovereignty. It galvanized the Moros'

aspiration for independence. Second, the pacification of the Huks involved large

distribution of Moro lands to Christian insurgents as reintegration incentive.[78]

The socio-political conditions during the Philippine-American War of 1899-1902,

parallel those of today's conflicts. America won the conventional war but was embroiled

in a bitter counterinsurgency conflict. U.S. soldiers battled elusive fighters in remote

jungles. The enemy used hit-and-run tactics to drain America's will. As the presidency

began to send additional troops, critics protested that the US could not afford to get

bogged down, and when the conflict was declared won, 4,196 American soldiers were

killed. This was the Philippine-American War which lasted from 1899 to 1902 but in this

conflict, the U.S. won.[79] However, a Muslim insurgency continued in the southern

Philippines for another decade and the actions taken then by the US acted as an

accelerant in today's counterinsurgency campaign in Mindanao.

The Moro Rebellion (1902 to 1913)

A defeated Spain ceded the Philippines to the US for $20 million in 1898 with the

Treaty of Paris. With the designation of the Philippines as a US Territory, and later a

Commonwealth, it ushered the loss of Moro independence. The Treaty officially forcibly annexed the Muslim Bangsamoro (Nation of Moro) located in the southern Philippines, now known as Mindanao. However, in order to buy time in prosecuting the Philippine-American War against the Filipino Christians in the northern Philippines, Brigadier General John C. Bates was sent to negotiate a treaty with the Sultan of Sulu in Mindanao. His main goal was to guarantee the Moros neutrality. The Bates Treaty was signed after negotiations with Sultan Jamalul Kiram II. It essentially made Sulu a US protectorate, with both sides mutually recognizing each others' sovereignty, and acknowledging that the Sultanate was independent of the Philippines.[80] Bates later admitted that the treaty was merely a stop-gap measure, signed only to buy time until the war in the north was ended and more forces could be brought to bear in the south.[81] To this day, Moro separatists refer to the Bates document as an international recognition of Bangsamoro independence. Consequently, the separatist rebellion by the Moros was sparked by the policy of the US in the aftermath of the Spanish-American War.

As planned, the US reneged on the Bates Treaty, after defeating the Filipino Christians in the northern Philippines, and immediately took action to absorb Sulu and Mindanao into the rest of the country. In 1904, the area was formed as the "Moro Province" of the Philippines under military governor General Leonard Wood. The simmering resentment of the American presence turned into a full-blown revolt known as the Moro Rebellion.[82] It would take until 1913 to quell the uprising and officially do away with the legal status of a separate Moro state in the Philippines; from that point the Moros lost their independence.[83] However, the Moros never gave up their aspiration for self-rule. The Muslim nationalist movement emerged out of this period of American

59

colonialism (1899 to 1946). Perhaps unintentionally, US colonial authorities actively encouraged its development by promoting a transcendent ethno-religious identity among Philippine Muslims. That unified identity then formed the basis of the nationalist Bangsamoro identity of the Muslim separatist movement.

American colonial intentions were complex, but a primary intention seems to have been to prepare Philippine Muslims for the eventual end of American colonialism and their inclusion in an independent Philippine republic as a consolidated and relatively progressive ethnic minority. But colonial practices did have the effect of encouraging the development of a unified Philippine Muslim (or Bangsamoro) identity.[84] Eventually, America granted the Philippines its independence in 4 July 1946 and Bangsamoro territories were incorporated into the new sovereign Philippine Republic. Accordingly, the government considered the Moros as Philippine citizens, including those fighting the government, that have equal rights and obligations with other Filipinos. However, to this present day, the Moros considered this as the illegal and immoral annexation of their homeland.

The Huk Rebellion (1946 to 1954)

Immediately following WWII, Americans and Filipinos joined forces, this time against a communist insurgency. From 1945 until 1955, the Philippine government, with American support, conducted one of the most successful counterinsurgency campaigns of the 20th Century against communist insurgents. The "Hukbalahap" or "Huk" guerilla force was formed in 1942.[85] Similar to the Malayan People's Anti-Japanese Army (MPAJA), the Huks originally formed in the Philippines to combat the Japanese occupation army. The term "Hukbalahap" is shorthand for "Hukbo ng Bayan Laban sa

Hapon" or in English "People's Army Against the Japanese."[86] After WWII, the Huks evolved into a communist organization whose grievance was rooted in the prevailing agricultural system which was essentially indentured servitude, an oppressive system imposed by the landed elites. This system with its inherent frustrations was described by the Commonwealth of the Philippines president, Manuel Quezon, in 1938 with:

> . . . as he works from sunrise to sundown, his employer gets richer while he remains poor. He has to drink the same polluted water his ancestors drank for ages. Malaria, dysentery, and tuberculosis still threaten him and his family at every turn. His children cannot go to school or if they do they cannot finish the whole primary instruction.[87]

General Douglas MacArthur saw the economic and social drivers of the Huks' discontent. At the close of WWII, his intelligence officer warned him that the Huks might attempt to impose a Soviet style government in the Philippines. However, MacArthur sympathized with the peasants and refused to send troop after the Huks by saying, "If I worked those sugar fields, I'd be a Huk myself."[88] However, MacArthur was also very loyal to his elite Filipino friends and left the status quo in their favor. Eventually, MacArthur left to command the occupation of Japan. The Huks laid down their arms and returned to work in the haciendas but not for long. They were once again mistreated socially and economically by the rich land owners, the country's elites.[89] However, this time the humiliation was no longer tolerated by the peasants. The Huks fought bravely in WWII and with the availability of weapons coupled with the nearing Philippine independence, the time was ripe to demand social change through a rebellion.[90]

The Huks' political goals were fairly straightforward. They wanted land ownership for peasants and "broadened democracy" in response to the corrupt national elections of 1946 and 1949. Their grievance was anchored in social justice and combating the prevailing corrupt political environment. The Huks continued to increase in strength and popularity from the end of WW II until 1951. In terms of military and political strength, some estimates listed the Huks at approximately 15,000 armed guerillas and approximately 1,000,000 sympathizers.[91]

At the center of government's innovative counterinsurgency campaign were a handful of individuals from diverse backgrounds. Most notable of the group were the Filipino Secretary of Defense, Ramon Magsaysay and Lieutenant Colonel Edward G. Lansdale,[92] advisor to Magsaysay. By chance these individuals were brought together at a critical time to provide key leadership in the Philippine efforts to defeat the Huk insurgency. Lansdale recognized that the Huk insurgency posed a growing threat to U.S interests in Asia. He immediately began to devise a plan to defeat the Huks, and enlisted the support and expertise of Filipino officers training in the U.S. It was during this time that Lansdale was introduced to Ramon Magsaysay who was then serving as a member of the Congress of the Philippines. Both recognized that the campaign would first and foremost be a battle for the hearts and minds of the Filipino population. Magsaysay and Lansdale recognized that support for communism was not a ringing endorsement for the Huk so much as a rejection of the existing Philippine government. Magsaysay noted three significant areas of concern. First, "the new democratic Philippine Government had drifted slowly toward what some people term the traditional Asian acceptance of inefficiency, graft, and corruption as the prerogatives of those in power." Secondly, abuse of citizens by the military. Finally, widespread and systemic poverty created feelings that the government was unconcerned for the plight of the average citizen.[93] Lansdale recognized that tactical victories cannot compensate for weak political objectives. He described the problem by stating, "The Huks were running a revolution and the Philippine government was fighting the Huks as though they were formal enemy armed forces."[94]

Magsaysay and Lansdale created a myriad of programs under the rubric of "civic action" which were designed to increase support for the government and military. These programs were perhaps the most significant tools in enabling the Philippine government to defeat the insurgency. Battalion commanders, civil affairs officers, and village leaders formed an effective triumvirate in planning security, agricultural improvements, and counter-guerrilla operations. Combat battalions provided much more than security. They also assisted in public works projects such as digging wells, building schools, and developing agricultural.[95] The Army also provided medical care and hospital support to civilians whom were injured by military actions. In another display of creativity and compassion, the Army provided military lawyers to represent tenant farmers in civilian court. Although Army lawyers had to appear in civilian clothes and the practice was conducted rather discretely. It still created a spirit of cooperation between soldiers and civilians. A Filipino journalist observed, "I have seen many armies but this one beats them all. This is an army with a social conscience."[96]

Perhaps the most innovative civic action program devised by the Philippine government was the Economic Development Corps (EDCOR). In December 1950, the EDCOR was created and placed under Magsaysay's leadership. It was designed to provide titled land and opportunity for reformed Huks in order to siphon off support for the Huk movement.[97] It provided an alternative to the Huks' stated goal of "land for the landless" by essentially providing low cost land to peasants that did not possess the financial resources to obtain land on their own. In 1951, the first two EDCOR communities were established in the Mindanao hinterland. Kapatagan was described as a "bandit-infested backland" and Buldon was established in an unpopulated jungle area.[98] An army unit of approximately company strength was placed in each village to provide security and assist in building infrastructure such as roads, schools, and housing. Additionally, the army provided legal support to assist settlers in obtaining the necessary land deeds and titles. The Army devoted substantial engineering efforts to water drainage, road construction, agricultural support, construction of infrastructure, and security. These civic action measures in the midst of Huk territory were credited with converting many Huk supporters. Lansdale stated, "many Huks surrendered, stating that they refused to fight against troops who were so helping the families of the Huks."[99] Nevertheless, significant kinetic and extensive intelligence operations continued against irreconcilable Huk units. However, According to Lansdale, Magsaysay personally believed that the civic action programs were "more decisive than the deployment of several battalion combat teams."[100] The campaign illustrates the overarching importance of utilizing military, economic, and informational programs in order to achieve legitimate political goals. Military operations were not viewed as the primary tool to facilitate the political objectives. The most important vehicle for success in this campaign was the hearts and minds effort that made the government earn legitimacy among its people through honest governmental elections, land reforms, and a spirit of cooperation and trust between security forces and the civilian population.[101]

As mentioned, the defeat of the Huks was primarily attributed to the government's successful comprehensive strategy led by EDCORs in the 1950s; agrarian reform through the distribution of land to the poor rebel peasants. Unfortunately, this successful heart and mind method, similar to the Bates Treaty, are contributing factors fueling the current Muslim insurgency in Mindanao since it was primarily Muslim ancestral lands in Mindanao that were given away and titled to Christian re-settlers from the northern Philippines, Luzon. This practice was continued by the Marcos regime in the 1970s to the Moros' detriment.

Today, Muslims are a minority in their own ancestral lands. Mindanao is roughly composed of 20 percent Muslim, with an 80 percent Christian majority, a countervailing force that is often opposed to Moro aspirations.[102] This is almost an exact opposite of Mindanao's demography a century ago. The Catholics majority believe that they should subjugate the Moros to their rule since the Moros are also Filipino who live in the same border and are entitled to the same rights, privileges, and national responsibilities. On the other hand, Moros continue to fight for self-determination and argue that they never agreed to be part of the Philippines and the Moro Sultanate government predates that of the Spanish colonization and American rule.

The modern Moro struggle for independence mutated into different factions. A lasting peace agreement continues to elude the Christian-led government and the Muslim minority. The constant mutation of the Muslim rebels into different splinter groups proves challenging in peace negotiations. Just when a peace agreement is reached, a splinter or breaks away group forms a new organization vowing to continue the armed struggle. In 1989 when the Moro National Liberation Front (MNLF) abandoned its separatist ambitions and agreed to the creation of the Autonomous Regions of Muslim Mindanao (ARMM), the Moro Islamic Liberation Front (MILF) splintered. In 2000, when the MILF sent feelers to the government to halt hostilities in exchange for a territorial expansion of the ARMM, the most violent splinter group formed, the Abu Sayyaf Group (ASG). The ASG and rogue elements of the MILF have ties to Jemaah Islamiyah (JI), a Southeast Asia terrorist network linked to Al-Qaeda and based in Indonesia. Today, a renewed ceasefire between MILF and the government is largely holding while the ASG is relentlessly hunted down and effectively diminished by the Armed Forces of the Philippines (AFP) with assistance from JSOTF-P.

At the request of the Government of the Philippines, JSOTF-P works alongside the AFP in support of Operation Enduring Freedom-Philippines (OEF-P). US service members are temporarily deployed to the Philippines in a strictly non-combat role to advise and assist the AFP. With the strength of no more than 600 personnel, JSOTF-P is composed of SOF and support personnel from all four branches of the U.S. military. JSOTF-P's mandate is to support the comprehensive approach of the AFP in their fight against terrorism in the southern Philippines and create the conditions necessary for peace, stability and prosperity. In other words, the AFP is conducting a counterinsurgency campaign while the JSOTF-P is conducting foreign internal defense (FID).[103]

The creation of JSOTF-P in the southern Philippines was preceded by a small-scale US military operation, shortly before the 11 September 2001 attack on America, intended to free the American missionary couple taken hostage by Abu Sayyaf Group (ASG) in 2001. On 27 May 2001, the ASG raid kidnapped about 20 people from Dos Palmas, an expensive resort on the island of Palawan, Philippines. The ASG considered three Americans as their most valuable hostages. They held hostage the missionary couple Martin and Gracia Burnham and Guillermo Sobero who was later beheaded by

ASG. The hostages and hostage-takers then returned hundreds of kilometer back across

the Sulu Sea to the ASG territories in Mindanao.[104] The region became a front in the

Global War on Terror (GWOT) when Washington and Manila set their sights on the

ASG's destruction. OEF-P officially began in early 2002 and is best known for Joint

Task Force (JTF) 510's combined US-RP operations on Basilan or Balikatan 02-1.[105] JTF

510 was the precursor to the much leaner JSOTF-P. With its long rebellious history,

dating close to 500 years, the Muslims in Mindanao were ripe for Al-Qaeda influence.

The Moros' discontent is rooted along ethnic, cultural, and religious fault-lines in a

region that has been only loosely controlled or governed throughout its long history of

occupation.[106] Mindanao has been continuously oppressed and neglected by the

Philippines' Christian majority, its lands exploited and given to Christian re-settlers.

Approximately five million Muslims live in five of the poorest provinces of the

Philippines. Mindanao is replete with multiple ungoverned and under-governed areas

where the government has nominal presence and much less control. These areas are

dominated by shadow governments where people live in fear. These areas are prime safe

havens for insurgents, terror groups, and criminal syndicates. According to Kalev Sepp:

> The security of the people must be assured as a basic need, along with
> food, water, shelter, health care, and a means of living. The failure of
> counterinsurgents and the root cause of insurgencies themselves can often be trace
> to government disregard of these basic rights.[107]

This is absolutely true in the case of Mindanao.

A close examination of the US strategy reveals close adherence to the

contemporary hearts and minds model based on the modernization and building the

legitimacy of the host nation's government. In the fight against terrorism, the JSOTF-P assists the AFP in bringing peace and prosperity in Mindanao. JSOTF-P works together

with the AFP to fight terrorism and deliver humanitarian assistance to the people of

Mindanao. US SOF are there to help strengthen the Philippines security forces, set the

conditions for good local governance, defeat terrorist organizations and protect US and

Philippine citizens from terrorist attacks.

At the invitation of the Philippine government the JSOTF-P assist the AFP as they

create a secure and stable environment. JSOTF-P's lines of operation are: capacity

building, civil military operations, information operations, and intelligence support

operations. These operations are based on proven strategies that have measurable effects.

> 1. *Capacity Building,* is training the AFP and the PNP to fight lawlessness.
> Villagers who once lived in fear of kidnapping for ransom and other criminal acts,
> now live in a more secure and peaceful environment. This increased capability
> provides improved security and allows the AFP and the PNP to increase the
> legitimacy of the government. For instance, the AFP has restricted the ASG's
> operational reach, once capable of striking Manila, to remote islands in the south.

> 2. *Civil Military Operations*, with the support from US Special Operations Forces,
> the AFP conducts civic action programs. Aside from providing security, they are
> armed with the tools and resources to rebuild schools and hospitals, provide
> medical (MEDCAPs), dental care (DENTCAPs), veterinary care (VETCAPs) and
> drill wells for fresh water.

> 3. *Information Operations*, it is building a connection between the government
> and the people. The cooperation of local citizens is vital in gathering the
> intelligence required to conduct operations against terrorists.

> 4. *Intelligence Support Operations*, US intelligence apparatus and systems are
> used in Mindanao to track Jemaah Islamiya (JI) and ASG high value targets
> (HVTs) and allow the AFP to neutralize these threats. Today, Philippine security
> forces had neutralized more than half of the terrorist on the HVTs list (Fig 4).
> Today, the hunt for terrorists continues.[108]

These are effective and proven operations that parallels those applied by the SAS

in Dhofar (table 1). Local people now see the AFP as a force for good, changing their lives for the better. It is creating a positive atmosphere of hope amongst the local

populace. But still it needs time and patience.

Table 1.   Lines of Operation Comparison between the British SAS
in Dhofar and those of JSOTF-P

SAS Dhofar (5) Lines of Operations (1970)	JSOTF-P Lines of Operations (2009)
To clearly identify the enemy and friendly forces by establishing an effective intelligence collection and collation system.	Intelligence Support Operations
To communicate clear intent to the insurgents, the population, and the government agencies and forces.	Information Operations
To provide security by helping the Dhofaris to protect their own province by involving them in the overall provision of security.	Capacity Building
To provide medical aid to the people of Dhofar in a region that had none.	Civil-military operations
To provide veterinary services for the cattle in the Dhofar region which are the main source of wealth.	Civil –military operations

Source: Created by author.

Silently entering its ninth year, JSOTF-P and the AFP partnership has had success

in reducing violence in Mindanao by gaining access to previously denied area, disrupting

terrorist operations, eliminating safe havens, and neutralizing insurgent leaders (see

figure 4). The hearts and minds approach is in the forefront of JSOTF-P's operation.

According to Col. Bill Coultrup, a previous JSOTF-P commander, his goal was simple,

"Help the Philippines security forces. It's their fight. We don't want to take over." Their

[US] work is only 20 percent combat-related and that portion of the military mission is

designed to "help the Armed Forces of the Philippines neutralize high-value targets--

individuals who will never change their minds," he said. Eighty percent of the effort,

69

though, has been "civil-military operations [CMO] to change the conditions that allow those high-value targets to have a safe haven," Coultrup added. "We do that through helping give a better life to the citizens through good governance, better health care, and a higher standard of living."[109] This hearts and minds strategy through Civil-Military Operations (CMO) is depicted in figure 5.

Figure 4.   Rewards for Justice HVT List
Source: US Embassy Manila, Philippines

70

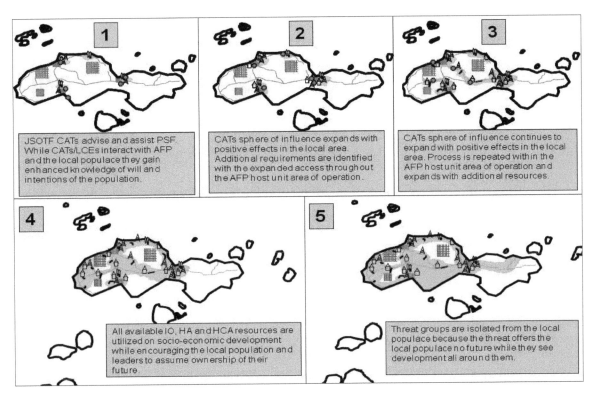

Figure 5.   JSOTF-P CMO Methodology

Source: Created by author.

Box 1- Red and white areas dominates both the physical and human terrain (AO).

Civil Affairs Teams (CATs) with their Philippines Security Forces (PSF) counterparts

conducts a civil reconassance and gather information in denied areas (influenced by

insurgents) in order to identify civil vulnerabilities or essential services the government is

failing to address. This is conducted through visual confirmation and local key leader

engagement (KLE).

Box 2- A foothold is gained and a small green area is established. Once civil

vulnerabilities are determined, these are prioritized and funding is requested. For

instance, if village has no clean water sources, a project nomination for a well is submitted by the CAT. In the meantime, the AFP re-engages the community with an easily executable civic action project with US resources and technical skills (e.g. MEDCAP, VETCAP) in order to establish rapport with residents.

Box 3- Green areas are expanding through continued local engagement and developing trust for PSF. As access improves and secutiy risk decreases, higher end CMO projects that were based on civil vulnerabilites are introduced. These are typically engineering civic action programs (ENCAPs) and entails water well drilling, school construction, clinic repairs, roads, governance centers, and markets.

Box 4- Green areas continues to expand while reducing the white areas and begin to isolate the red areas. All assets are put to bare in order to maximize the effects of these civic action prorams. Public Affairs, Information Operations and Military Information Suport Operations works to spread the word, creates a perception of progress, and steps in Boxes 1-3 are repeated elsewhere.

Box 5- Red areas are isolated causing separation between insurgents and population, reduced white areas denies insurgents mobility. The population sees their government as a force for good and life is better. They make a cost benefit analysis, hedge their bets, and sees that the government have more to offer than the insurgents.

Lessons Learned

Nevertheless, considering JSOTF-P's successful partnership with the AFP, it has had challenges and offers numerous lessons:

Alternate Local Government

A challenge with CMO success is that you become another shadow government. Locals are aware that with US forces come US dollars. Locals are cognizant that the sudden influx of progress though CMO projects are funded by the Americans. As such, local officials and politicians come straight to JSOTF-P for assistance or political legitimacy. This could undermine the legitimacy of the host nation government. In the politically-charged Philippine environment, great care is taken to redirect assistance requested by the people to their government and at the same time not offend anyone. Every CMO projects is never neutral. You are either affecting the insurgents or causing project envy from other political clans.

Dependency

Although always well intended, CMO projects could create dependency. In the rush to portray progress or spend year-end dollars, an influx of projects are executed. For instance, in one island in Mindanao, JSOTF-P spent on development more than the local government. Taking the island's poverty into consideration, this was almost inevitable. Case in point, at a reception following a ribbon cutting ceremony for a newly built airstrip funded by America's dollars, a high ranking local government official approached the author and whispered, "So Matt, when you are building my seaport?"[110]

To a certain extent, this dependency permeates the local security forces and stymied professional growth. The US forces' are typically on a six to nine-month deployments. This generates a compulsion to hit the ground running, a rush to achieve, and to create attributable achievements/projects to one's deployment. This fast pace tempo is often desynchronized with that of the local forces'. They operate at a slower pace due to the fact that they have been fighting this war for over 40 years. Consequently, there have been several incidents where US forces acted unilaterally. They conceived, planned, and funded an entire project with minimal or no input from or participation by local forces. Afterwards, in a rush to put a 'Filipino face' to the initiative, local security forces and politicians are placed center stage for the inauguration or ribbon cutting ceremony at the last minute. Full credit is given to local military and civilian authorities and US contribution is downplayed. This misplaced interpretation of 'by, through, and with' places emphasis on results rather than process. It is contrary to capacity building and creates a level of dependency.

Stability versus Development

Addressing civil vulnerabilities is part of stability operations. These are causes of suffering that plant the seeds of discontent where the insurgents find an ideological same haven. In Mindanao, civil vulnerabilities are in abundance due to the decades of intentional neglect by the government services that are expected from the government-- security, water, electricity, academics (or schools), transportation, medical, and sanitation (SWEAT-MS). Though one of the best US interagency relationships can be found in the Philippines between JSOTF-P and USAID (Manila), this was not the always the case. There was an initial conflict of interest between the two organizations. An initial friction point was the manner US humanitarian activities are funded and executed in country. Through their Growth in Mindanao (GEM)[111] programs, USAID requires a minimum percent buy-in from local communities for projects. This is a proven model that promotes local ownership to projects. While on the other hand, JSOTF-P funded projects 100 percent. Consequently, locals prefer to have JSOTF-P construct their projects.

Conversely, instead of creating synergy through complementing efforts an unintentional competition exited.

The disconnect lies in the dichotomy of objectives between the organizations. JSOTF-P was looking at immediate results that will stabilize the environment while USAID was in it for long-term development. JSOTF-P's projects were meant to gain quick access to denied communities, disrupt lawlessness, and deny sanctuaries. Asking or negotiating for local contribution would delay operations while USAID, and rightfully so, will ask for local project buy-in to ensure projects will be taken cared of for a long time. Eventually, JSOTF-P adjusted its operations and when possible does ask local governments to contribution in kind or labor. JSOTF-P and USAID projects were synchronized and both organizations exchanged liaison officers.

Building Little Americas

Initially, JSOTF-P had minimal tactical patience and relied heavily on results based on an American timeline. This is contrary to building a host nation's capacity by increasing its capabilities. The US approach was on getting things done when the process should have been more important. JSOTF-P fell into one of the intellectual challenges mentioned in the beginning of the thesis, the preconceived notion of modernization. US planners are familiar with modernity and get trapped on predetermined ideas about what needs and grievances to address rather than to actually listen to the local population. By way of example, civil affairs planners were funded and approved to build a four-structure community center for every municipality in one of the islands. The island hand 18 municipalities and one community center costs $120,000 for a total of $2,160,000 in a span of three years. After a few were completed the author, who recently arrived in

75

country, decided to check one of these highly praised community centers. The visit

proved dreadful. The author discovered that the center, which is barely a year old, was

dilapidated, with holes on the roof, fixtures stolen, and one building turned into an animal

stable. It was evidently not kept or used for its intended purpose. The author visited the

provincial leader responsible for this project for an explanation. The reply was eye

opening:

> The design of the buildings is one issue, I have discussed it with you [previous unit] but you were so keen on your US design and concept. So, expect many other ACC building that will just be left in the open, another white elephant. Sometimes, if not all the time, sincere donors have to have the ears and heart for their development partners, we are not mere beneficiaries of your projects, we are partners.[112]

In other words, the Americans fell in love with their own plans and failed to listen

to population, the people who will eventually use the facility. Only the local people

would know what is best for them. After engaging the same provincial officer but this

time with a team that was receptive to local ideas, the reply was:

> Thank you for the humility that you have, I think you got my points well. We wanted to make things work for Sulu. The development initiatives should not be solely for development alone, it should be geared towards peace building. I would like to believe that peace can be achieved if we have the same sincerity, humility, empathy and framework.[113]

Leveraging Religion

JSOTF-P funds are not authorized to engage religious structures and activities.

According to a senior Civil Affairs officer currently deployed in the Philippines:

> You cannot use any funds to fund a mosque or other religious related activities. There have been instances where repairs have been made to mosques for battle damages, or if they were openly available to the general public as a community center.[114]

This is a missed powerful avenue of influence. Religion permeates every activity in Mindanao. It is what makes the Muslim residents of the region different from the rest of the Filipino Christian majority. CMO dollars should not be viewed primarily for development and humanitarian reasons only. It should be considered first and foremost a tool for influence, to advance military objectives. If a community is asking for their mosque to be refurbished but you gave them a town hall instead, how much rapport and leverage did you build with the community?[115] Do you think the dollars were spent wisely to achieve a military end? Do you think they will value the new structure and maintain it?

Condition Based Civic Action Programs

Finally, CMO projects must not be based on the expected gratitude and anticipated reciprocity for kindness rendered. CMO activities effectiveness should not be based on hope and prayer but on conditions. Before a project breaks ground, a dialogue must be made with the local population's key leaders and expectations should be articulated. For instance, a village needs a well and it has been determined that this village has tactical value for it is a known insurgent transient point. The condition could be that the AFP-JSOTF-P will fund a well provided that insurgents will be denied access to the village if not reported immediately. If insurgent traffic does not subside and government forces are ambushed in the area, the well will be capped permanently. This was an important lesson in Dhofar. CMO projects must be conditions based thereby forcing the population to choose irrevocably. Even more significant is for the counterinsurgents to have the tactical will to follow through and cap the well if trust if broken. This will win the population's respect and highlight the importance of the CMO

77

activity. Most people are conditioned to respect authority. If you are kind but perceived weak, you will not win the population.[116]

But the Philippine case study cannot become a one-size-fits-all template for other insurgencies. The Philippines political and economic circumstances, history and relationship with the United States differ vastly from Iraq or Afghanistan. In most respects, the Philippines is an atypical case. The Philippines government, military, and education system is in America's image. Many Filipinos know the US well. Numerous Philippine presidents were educated in the US and Filipinos value greatly an American education. For instance, former President Fidel V. Ramos is from the 1950 West Point Class while Gloria Macapagal-Arroyo was classmates with Bill Clinton in Georgetown University. In addition, a lot of Filipinos have relatives living in America. Large numbers have served in the US armed forces. Their personal familiarity enhances and facilitates cooperation. The Philippines possesses a functioning constitutional democracy, an organized military, and the Muslim insurgents are confined to the southern islands of Mindanao.[117] The US and the Philippines has had a long love-hate relationship that began in the turn of the 20th century. Nevertheless, its friendship has survived the test of time and the Philippines, predicatively, will remain America's ally in Southeast Asia; a testament to America's previous and continuing hearts and minds successes in the Philippines.

Afghanistan

The decisive terrain is the human terrain. The people are the center of gravity. Only by providing them security and earning their trust and confidence can the Afghan government and ISAF prevail.[118]

— General Petraeus

Protecting the Afghan people is the mission. The Afghan people will decide who wins this fight, and we (GIROA and ISAF) are in the struggle for their support. The effort to gain and maintain that support must inform every action we take. Essentially, we and the insurgents are presenting an argument for the future to the people of Afghanistan; they will decide which argument is the most attractive, most convincing, and has the greatest success.[119]

— General McChrystal

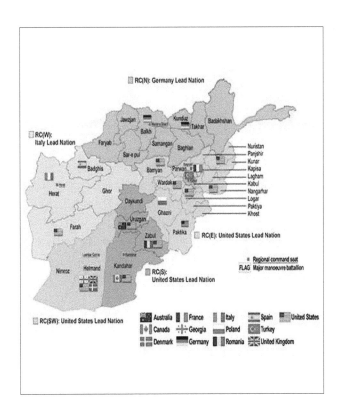

Figure 6.   Map of Afghanistan with ISAF contributing nations

Source: usacac.army.mil

The Al Qaeda attacks on 11 September 2001 caught America by surprise. With a death toll nearing 3,000, this attack on American soil was more costly than that inflicted by the Japanese at Pearl Harbor in 7 December 1941.[120] America had to act. A decision was made to wage a war in Afghanistan in order to end the Taliban government's safe haven to Al Qaeda. In 26 days, US troops were prosecuting the war on the ground. The Taliban was overthrown before the year ended. Following the initial US and Afghan forces' success, an increasingly violent insurgency began to develop. A mixed group of insurgents comprised of the Taliban, Hezb-i-Islami, the Haqqani network, foreign fighters, local tribes, and criminal organizations began a sustained effort to overthrow the Afghan government.[121] To date, entering its tenth year, the Afghan conflict is the longest in America's history and still continues to rage.

Today, under the banner of the North Atlantic Treaty Organization (NATO) and with 48 contributing nations,[122] the US-led International Security Assistance Force (ISAF) is in support of the Government of the Islamic Republic of Afghanistan (GIROA). Its stated mission is to conduct operations in Afghanistan to reduce the capability and will of the insurgency, support the growth in capacity and capability of the Afghan National Security Forces (ANSF), and facilitate improvements in governance and socio-economic development, in order to provide a secure environment for sustainable stability that is observable to the population.[123] ISAF is supporting reconstruction and development (R&D) in Afghanistan, securing areas in which reconstruction work is conducted by other national and international actors. Where appropriate, and in close cooperation and coordination with GIROA and United Nations Assistance Mission in Afghanistan (UNAMA) representatives on the ground, ISAF is also providing practical support for

R&D efforts, as well as support for humanitarian assistance efforts conducted by Afghan government organizations, international organizations, and NGOs.[124] ISAF, through its Provincial Reconstruction Teams (PRT), is helping the Afghan authorities strengthen the institutions required to establish good governance and rule of law and to promote human rights. The PRTs' principal mission consists of building [local governments'] capacity, supporting the growth of governance, structures and promoting an environment within which governance can improve.[125]

Much of the discussion of the Afghan campaign focuses of the importance of winning hearts and minds of the Afghan people but in reality it is just as important to the campaign's ultimate success to win the hearts and minds in the domestic populations of the coalition's participants.[126] Although the history of the Afghan conflict is still being written, some observers have stated that the counterinsurgency campaign in Afghanistan is just beginning, dismissing the previous eight years as marred by a lack of coherent strategy, and insufficient resources to implement an effective counterinsurgency.[127]

Infusion of Western Concepts

Evident by the opening quotes, the current ISAF Commander, General H. David Petraeus, and his predecessor, General Stanley A. McChrystal, believe that the security of and winning the Afghan population's support is at the core of ISAF's counterinsurgency campaign. However, earning the population's support through the contemporary hearts and minds approach will prove difficult. Afghanistan's tribal system, xenophobic culture, and tumultuous history will challenge Western-based modernization theory and legitimacy approach that exists today. Winning hearts and minds of the local population in order to remove the support base of insurgents is different from the attempt to establish a perception of legitimacy of international presence and revolutionary political and societal changes instigated by the international community in Afghanistan. According to Anatol Lieven, "ancient cultural traditions have always inclined many Afghans and Pashtuns in particular, to resist state power."[128] He also argues that resisting foreign occupation is part of the "Pashtun Way" and that the insurgency in Afghanistan has to be understood as largely inevitable given its cultural predisposition. He adds, "In view of the history of Pashtun resistance to outside military conquest over the past 150 years, it would on the contrary be nothing short of astonishing if massive insurgency had not occurred."[129] These conditions and forced modernization creates a difficult challenge in winning the population. It is creating an unintentional contradiction to ISAF's objectives.

The narrow Western interpretation of legitimacy that is bounded by Jeffersonian democratic concepts, clashes with other indigenous forms of governance. The traditional sources of legitimacy in Afghanistan often based on identity and cultural affinity produce major problems for prescriptive counterinsurgency plans. A broader understanding of legitimacy and the way it operates within the specific culture, like Afghanistan, is necessary in order to create informed strategies, and possibly to lower ambitions. The international coalition is considered an unwelcome outside presence with values foreign to rural Afghans. These foreigners are the proponents of imposing an alien and highly suspicious centralized system of governance that is manifested in the unpopular Karzai government. Consequently, this creates a steep uphill battle to legitimacy which cannot be won by incremental improvements in the economic and social situation of certain Afghans while continuously failing to provide the most basic services of security and justice.[130]

The significant challenge is whether the international community can have the flexibility and conviction to deviate from the Western principles of good governance and modernization. Legitimacy is a question of values by which different groups in society would perceive the government system as legitimate or illegitimate based on how well their own values matched with that of the system.[131] Legitimacy is thereby inherently subjective and evaluated in what the population regards as legitimate or illegitimate according to the way a political system fit their values. If a main objective is to win hearts and minds through legitimacy, reforms and activities should then imitate existing values and perceptions of what legitimate governance is to the many ethnic groupings of Afghans.

SAS veterans from Dhofar said that they were puzzled and humored when political pundits boast about the Afghanistan election. They feel they are a waste of time.[132] Similar to the Adoo, Western governance is an alien concept to the Afghans. They have their own history of governance and style of tribal democracy. The British counterinsurgency efforts in Malaya and Dhofar did not impose a new system of government or a new social order but allowed the people to maintain traditional political and social structures. The establishment of Western norms of governance to win hearts and minds presents a crisis of legitimacy as it starts out by tearing down the existing structures of power sharing; thereby, threatening the power and status of existing power holders.[133]

The local population's perceptions of the insurgent and counterinsurgent are important in deciding which side to support. If the traditional systems of governance and justice command higher levels of legitimacy than the new system that is introduced, the campaign is in jeopardy. Alexis de Tocqueville's *Democracy in America* provides an

excellent description of loss of legitimacy:

> . . . epochs sometimes occur in the life of a nation when the old customs of a
> people are changed, public morality is destroyed, religious belief shaken, and the
> spell of tradition broken . . . leaving the citizens with neither the instinctive
> patriotism of new monarchy nor the reflecting patriotism of a republic . . . they
> have stopped between the two in the midst of confusion and distress.[134]

This parallels the current political situation in Afghanistan. Kilcullen accurately notes

that in many conflicts the counterinsurgent actually represents revolutionary change,

"while the insurgents fight to preserve the status quo of ungoverned spaces, or to repel an

occupier, a political relationship opposite to that envisaged in classical

counterinsurgency."[135] This is precisely what is happening in certain parts of Afghanistan

where not only traditional values command higher legitimacy, but also the Taliban

insurgency is managing the struggle for hearts and minds quite well with their shadow

structures of government, emphasizing security and justice by traditional means. The

revolutionary insertion of alien norms of governance risks eroding the potential

legitimacy of the international presence, as well as of the host government.[136]

In November 2009, Malalai Joya, a former member of the Afghan Parliament and

the author of *Raising My Voice*, expressed opposition to an expansion of the U.S. military

presence in Afghanistan and concern about the future of her country:

> Eight years ago, the U.S. and NATO--under the banner of women's rights, human
> rights, and democracy--occupied my country and pushed us from the frying pan
> into the fire. Eight years is enough to know better about the corrupt, mafia system
> of President Hamid Karzai. My people are crushed between two powerful
> enemies. From the sky, occupation forces bomb and kill civilians . . . and on the
> ground, the Taliban and warlords continue their crimes. It is better that they leave
> my country; my people are that fed up. Occupation will never bring liberation and
> it is impossible to bring democracy by war.[137]

While the economic and governance issues should certainly not be dismissed, a broader understanding of what commands legitimacy means that ethnic identity and dynamics, as well as other aspects of traditional systems of governance will have to be included in a sound counterinsurgency strategy.[138]

Dependency and Corruption

The Afghan insurgency is primarily based on ethnic tensions, poor governance, and economic difficulties, all these have been rallying points for disaffected Afghans.[139] ISAF has in its campaign plan the aim of extending the reach of the Afghan government. The PRT's primary purpose is to deliver reconstruction, governance, and security to the local population under the auspices of the Afghan central government.[140] Most of the development tasks are performed by the PRTs, which generally include Western civilian staff as political and development advisors. The strategy of the PRT is to extend the central government's reach and create zones of stability that will win over local people and then expand, otherwise known as the ink blot method, and gradually, through a thousand successful blots, cover the bulk of the country. However, similar to the challenge articulated earlier in the Philippines, success does create a dependency or the PRTs and the population gravitates towards the PRTs consequently creating a shadow government instead of building the legitimacy and capacity of the local government. Afghan officials and even President Karzai have accused PRTs of virtually establishing parallel governments.[141] This is detrimental to long term stability. The local governmental processes, even if viewed inefficient in Western standards, must be harnessed and allowed to build its capacity.

The challenge with the central Afghan government is not that is does not have the reach but that it is corrupt and oppressive. Coalition veterans from Afghanistan interviewed for the Scholars program, expressed frustration in regards to the varying degrees of corruption in the Afghan central government. Several highlighted the corruption in the construction projects from nepotistic awarding to bogus companies competing for bids. A local government official was quoted that developed dollars are schemed in four occasions: during the bidding process, application for building permits, construction, and ribbon-cutting ceremony. In other words, development projects are corrupted from start to finish.[142] In 2010, Afghanistan slipped three places in Transparency International's annual index of corruption perceptions, becoming the world's third most-corrupt country ahead of just Myanmar and Somalia.[143]

If you are going to succeed in the counterinsurgency governance contest, you have to deliver to the people legitimate, responsive, just and effective government at the local level. It is not enough to be effective, you have to be just. Justice, or fairness, is probably right now the most important aspect for the Afghan population. People are not happy with the Taliban; however, some see them as more fair and just than the Afghan government.[144] This clearly erodes the host nation's legitimacy. Ambassador Karl W. Eikenberry, a retired three-star general who in 2006-2007 commanded U.S. troops in Afghanistan, and is now the US Ambassador to Afghanistan, also expressed frustration with the relative paucity of funds set aside for spending on development and reconstruction in Afghanistan.[145] In subsequent cables, Ambassador Eikenberry repeatedly cautioned that deploying sizable American reinforcements would result in astronomical costs--tens of billions of dollars--and would only deepen the dependence of the Afghan government on the United States. Two years later, July 2009, Eikenberry states, "It remains to be seen whether Karzai can or will refrain from this 'blame America' tactic he uses to deflect criticism of his administration. . . . Indeed, his inability to grasp the most rudimentary principles of nation-building and his deep seated insecurity as a leader combines to make any admission of fault unlikely, in turn confounding our best efforts to find in Karzai a responsible partner."[146]

Aid and Instability

The contemporary interpretation of winning hearts and minds in a setting of comprehensive approaches to stabilization and peace building have, according to Andrew Wilders[147] created a number of questionable assumptions regarding the links between stabilization and aid. First, he challenges the assumption that development and modernization efforts have stabilizing effects on a conflict. It is anchored on the idea that aid dollars generate economic growth that propels development and eventually creates stability. One of the main rationales given for the assumed link between aid and security is the belief that poverty is a major factor fueling the insurgency. This has become a centerpiece of American counterinsurgency strategy. "Where the road ends, the Taliban begins,"[148] said General Eikenberry in 2006, and Vice President Biden declared in 2008, "How do you spell hope in Pashto and Dari? A-S-P-H-A-L-T."[149] Development actors have also embraced the idea that poverty breeds radicalism. Since 9/11 the money for development has grown dramatically, and much of those funds have been directed to peace building activities.[150] Yet Wilder argues that there is little evidence that poverty, inadequate infrastructure, or the lack of social services are major factors driving the insurgency in either Afghanistan or Pakistan. In fact, some of the poorest and least developed regions of Afghanistan are actually the most stable. The poorest areas of

Pakistan are rural Baluchistan, rural Sindh, and southern Punjab--not the Federally

Administered Tribal Areas (FATA)[151] where the Pakistani Taliban are based.[152]

Next, Wilder challenges assumption that aid projects help win the hearts and

minds and thereby increase support for the host government and the international

presence. He asserts that rapid increase in foreign aid combined with Afghanistan state

institutions' inability to effectively spend and account for these funds fuels corruption. It

is eroding the very legitimacy it is trying to instill. In interviews with Afghans in five

provinces (Helmand, Paktia, Orozgan, Farah, and Balkh) Wilder asked three questions,

"What are the drivers of instability, what do you think about development actors, and

does development help with insecurity?" The answers revealed that perceptions of aid

actors were mostly negative, with little distinction between NGOs, the military, and

government ministries. The common complaints were unmet expectations and broken

promises, unfair distributions, corruption, inappropriate or shoddy projects, and lack of

consultation. For example, building a road angered those who it bypassed, while the haste

and lack of oversight in the construction might mean that it is already crumbling, while

the PRT that built it has already transferred out of the country.

The most destabilizing effect of aid, however, is its role in fueling massive

corruption, which in turn is eroding the legitimacy of the government.[153] In Paktia

province, where the US-led PRT has been funding aid projects since 2003, a tribal elder

explained:

> Paktia has lots of problems, but the issue of lack of clinics, schools, and
> roads are not the problem. The main problem is we don't have a good
> government. . . . Without a clean government, millions of dollars are stolen. If you

increase the amount of money it will also be useless because the government will simply steal more. There's a growing distance between the people and the government and this is the main cause of the deteriorating security situation.[154]

The Taliban exploits this sentiment, and seeks to legitimize its movement by promising better security, quick justice, and a less corrupt government, rather than more roads, schools, and clinics.

Within the military, the assumption that aid wins hearts and minds is reinforced by the Army's publication of the *Commanders Guide to Money as a Weapons System.* Not since the Civil Operations and Revolutionary Development Support (CORDS)[155] program in Vietnam has aid so explicitly been viewed as a "weapons system," especially in counterinsurgency. This April 2009 publication provides guidance on how to use money and opens with:

> Warfighters at brigade, battalion, and company level in a counterinsurgency environment employ money as a weapons system to win the hearts and minds of the indigenous population to facilitate defeating the insurgents. Money is one of the primary weapons used by warfighters to achieve successful mission results in counterinsurgency and humanitarian operations.[156]

In fact, several interviewed officers admitted that they felt pressured to spend on projects. Officer performance rating schemes were tied to dollars spent and number of projects built. The number of ribbon-cutting ceremonies was a gauge for activity and effectiveness rather than measuring the actual impact of that money spent. Still there is very little evidence that development assistance is effectively winning hearts and minds and promoting US security objectives.[157]

Wilder's research in Afghanistan indicates that the empirical evidence suggest that non-coercive hearts and minds approach may be false.[158] Ultimately, his research showed that perceptions of massive corruption and the failure of the state to promote security and the rule of law were much more important factors in delegitimizing the state than its failure to deliver adequate levels of social services or infrastructure. It suggests that the international community is hindered in winning Afghan hearts and minds not because it spends too little money, but because it has spent too much too quickly, often in insecure environments with extremely limited implementation and oversight capacity. For instance, most of the US development aid is spent in the insecure areas of the south and southeast, with relatively little going to the more secure central and northern regions (leading Afghans in those areas to complain bitterly about the "peace penalty").[159] In an ethnically and tribally divided society like Afghanistan, aid can also easily generate jealousy and ill will by inadvertently helping to consolidate the power of some tribes or factions at the expense of others, often pushing rival groups into the arms of the Taliban.

The Taliban seem to recognize this, and seek to legitimize their movement by promising better security, justice and governance rather than more roads, schools and clinics.[160] While the extent of the problem is difficult to gauge, it is likely that US foreign aid is becoming an increasingly important source of financing for the Taliban as more and more CERP and USAID money is contracted out to construction companies to work in insecure areas. A recent article in *The Nation* quoted a U.S. military official in Kabul who estimated, "a minimum of 10 percent of the Pentagon's logistics contracts–hundreds of millions of dollars–consists of payments to insurgents."[161] The lack of control measures in massive aid influx is fueling corruption due to laxness in fiscal accountability. For example, there have been numerous reports of the Taliban being paid protection money by donor-funded contractors, especially for their road building projects.

By paying the Taliban, local contractors buy the safety of their workers, equipment, and prevent attacks on projects.[162]

[1]For an in-depth study of the Malayan Emergency, the author recommends: Richard Stubbs, "From Search and Destroy to Hearts and Minds: The Evolution of British Strategy in Malaya 1948-60," in *Counterinsurgency in Modern Warfare,* eds. Daniel Marston and Carter Malkasian, 2010, 101-118; Robert Komer, *The Malayan Emergency in Retrospect: Organization of a Successful Counterinsurgency Effort* RAND, 1972, 25-68; John Coates, *Suppressing Insurgency*, 1992, 77-108; Daniel Marston, "Lost and Found in the Jungle," in *Big Wars and Small Wars,* ed. Hew Strachan, 2006, 96-114; Wade Markel, "Draining the Swamp: The British Strategy of Population Control," *Parameters* (Spring 2006), 35-48; Brigadier M. C. A. Henniker, *Red Shadow Over Malaya*, 1955, 61-70; Leon Comber, *Malaya's Secret Police 1945-1960: The Role of the Special Branch in the Malayan Emergency*, 2009, 173-217; Richard Miers, *Shoot to Kill*, 1959, 159-173.

[2]Cloake, *Templer: Tiger of Malaya. The Life of Field Marshal Sir Gerald Templer*, 262.

[3]Dixon, "Hearts and Minds," 366.

[4]The MNLA was partly a re-formation of the Malayan People's Anti-Japanese Army (MPAJA), the MCP-led guerrilla force which had been the principal resistance in Malaya against the Japanese occupation. The British had secretly trained and armed the MPAJA during the later stages of World War II.

[5]British Document End of Empire (BDEE) The Situation in Malaya. Cabinet Memorandum. 1 July 1948, 41.

[6]BDEE. Federation Plan for Elimination of the MCP in Malaya. The Briggs Plan. 24th May 1950, 216.

[7]Subsequently British introduced the emergency regulation throughout the Malaya Federation to take effect on 18 June 1948. (BDEE), Declaration of Emergency. Telegram No 641 from Sir E. Gent to Mr. Creech Jones, 17 June 1948.

[8]BDEE. The Situation in Malaya. Cabinet Memorandum, 1 July 1948, 40.

[9]Ibid., 41.

[10]Richard L. Clutterbuck, *The Long, Long War: Counterinsurgency in Malaya and Vietnam* (New York: Frederick A. Praeger, 1966), 206.

[11]Philip Deery, "Malaya, 1948: Britain's Asian Cold War?" (Working Paper, International Center for Advance Studies, New York University, April 2002), 25.

[12]Stanley Bedlington, *Malaysia and Singapore: The Building of New States* (Ithaca: Cornell University Press, 1978), 78.

[13]Robert W. Komer, "The Malayan Emergency in Retrospect: Organization of a Successful Counterinsurgency Effort" (Report, Advanced Research Projects Agency, RAND Corporation, Santa Monica, CA, 1972), http://www.rand.org/ pubs/reports/R957/ (accessed 20 November 2010), vi.

[14]The initial counterinsurgency plan was ineffective. Prior to Briggs appointment as Director of Operations, the Army used large-scale sweeps which provided the insurgent sufficient warning to disappear in the jungle. This frustrated the military that led to civilian abuses and atrocities. The Army appeared more at war with the population instead of acting as its protector. (Richard Stubbs, "From Search and Destroy to Hearts and Minds" in *Counterinsurgency in Modern Warfare*, eds. Daniel Marston et al., 2010, 103).

[15]Jerome F. Bierly and Timothy W. Pleasant, "Malaya-A Case Study," *Marine Corps Gazette* 74 (July 1990), 48.

[16]David Galula, *Counterinsurgency Warfare: Theory and Practice.* (Saint Petersburg, FL: Glenwood Press, 1964), 102

[17]Riley Sunderland, *Organizing Counterinsurgency in Malaya: 1947-1960* (Santa Monica, CA: RAND Corporation, 1964), 64.

[18]Komer, "The Malayan Emergency in Retrospect," 33.

[19]Ibid.

[20]BDEE. Federation Plan for Elimination of the MCP in Malaya, The Briggs Plan, 24 May 1950, 216.

[21]James Corum, Training Indigenous Forces in Counterinsurgency: A Tale of Two Insurgencies. 1 March 2006, http://www.strategicstudiesinstitute.army. mil/pubs/display.cfm?PubID=648 (accessed 13 November 2010), 36,

[22]James P. Ongkili, *Nation-building in Malaysia 1946–1974* (Singapore: Oxford University Press, 1985), 79.

[23]Komer, "The Malayan Emergency in Retrospect," 17.

[24]Corum, Training Indigenous Forces in Counterinsurgency, 189.

[25]The FARELF Training Center (FTC) in KotaTingi, Malaysia was known to the soldiers as the Jungle Training Center.

[26]Small Wars Journal, 11 November 2010.

[27]Wade Markel, "Draining the Swamp: The British Strategy of Population Control," *Parameters* (Spring 2006): 39.

[28]Sunderland, *Winning the Heart and Minds of the People*, 20.

[29]Kalev I. Sepp, "Best Practices in Counterinsurgency," *Military Review* (May - June 2005): 8.

[30]Dixon, "Hearts and Minds," 454.

[31]Markel, "Draining the Swamp," 44.

[32]BDEE, White Area in Malacca, 28 Aug 1953. White Area are districts declared clear of insurgents or eliminated and the Emergency Regulations withdrawn.

[33]Ibid.

[34]The Government White Paper Report, *The Militant Communist Threat to Malaysia*. (Kuala Lumpur: National Press,1966): 16.

[35]David Benest, "Aden to Northern Ireland, 1966-76," in *Big Wars and Small Wars: The British Army and the Lessons of War in the Twentieth Century*, ed. Hew. Strachan (London: Routledge, 2006), 118-19.

[36]Markel, "Draining the Swamp," 44, 47.

[37]One of the most notorious atrocities of the conflict was the Batang Kali massacre. It took place on 12 December 1948 during British military operations against native communists. The 7th Plt, G Company, 2nd Scots Guard surrounded a rubber estate at Sungai Rimoh, Batang Kali, Selangor and shot 24 villagers before setting fire to the village. Only one adult male survived who was presumed dead by the Guardsmen. The men had been separated from the women and children for interrogation before the shooting began. The incident today is sometimes described as Britain's *My Lai* massacre.

[38]David Anderson, *Histories of the Hanged: Britain's Dirty War in Kenya and the End of Empire* (London: Phoenix, 2005); Huw Bennett, "The Other Side of the COIN: Minimum and Exemplary Force in British Army Counterinsurgency in Kenya," *Small Wars and Insurgencies* 18, no. 4 (December 2007): 638-64.

[39]David Martin Jones and M. L. R. Smith, "Whose Hearts and Whose Minds? The Curious Case of Global Counter-Insurgency," *The Journal of Strategic Studies* 33 (February 2010): 97.

[40]Neil Sheehan, *A Bright Shining Lie: John Paul Vann and America in Vietnam* (New York: Random House, 1988), 309-310; Sam Castan, "Vietnam's Two Wars," *Look*, 28 January 1964, 32-36; Kuno Knoebl, *Victor Charlie* (New York: Frederick A. Praegar Publishers, 1967), 257.

[41]Dixon, "Heart and Minds," 366.

[42]Karl Hack, "Screwing Down the People: The Malayan Emergency, Decolonisation and Ethnicity," in *Imperial Policy and Southeast Asian Nationalism*, eds. H. Antlov and S. Tonnesson (Richmond, UK: Curzon Press, 1995), 95.

[43]For an in-depth study of the Dhofar Rebellion, the author recommends: Ian Beckett, "The British Counter-insurgency Campaign in Dhofar, 1965-1975," in *Counterinsurgency in Modern Warfare,* eds. Daniel Marston and Carter Malkasian, 2010, 175-190; Bard O'Neill, "Revolutionary War in Oman" in *Insurgency in the Modern World*, 1980, 213-234; D. L. Price, *Oman: Insurgency and Development* (London: Institute for the Study of Conflict, 1975), 1-19; Tony Jeapes, *SAS: Operation Oman* (London: William Kimber, 1980), 15-31 and 207-237; and Walter Ladwig III, "Supporting Allies in COIN: Britain and the Dhofar Rebellion," *Small Wars and Insurgencies* 19 no. 1 (March 2008): 62-88.

[44]T. E. Lawrence, "Twenty-Seven Articles," *The Arab Bulletin*, 20 August 1917.

[45]Tony Jeapes, *SAS: Operation Oman* (London: William Kimber and CO, 1980), 237.

[46]Best literature for recommendation.

[47]Walter Ladwig III, "Supporting Allies in COIN: Britain and the Dhofar Rebellion," *Small Wars and Insurgencies* 19, no. 1 (March 2008): 77.

[48]CGSC Scholars Program 2010, Dhofar Veterans Panel.

[49]Command and General Staff College Scholars Program 2010, *Scholars Program Counterinsurgency Research Study 2010.* (Fort Leavenworth, KS: Ike Skelton Chair in Counterinsurgency, 2010); personal correspondence with Paul Sibley, author of *A Monk in the SAS.*

[50]Ibid.

[51]Ibid.

[52]Ibid.

[53]Fred Halliday, *Arabia Without Sultans* (New York: Vintage Books, 1997), 325-326.

[54]The Jebel referred in this thesis pertains to the rugged hills in Dhofar and not to be confused with the more imposing Jebel mountain ranges on the northeastern end Oman vicinity of the capital Muscat.

[55]Ladwig, "Supporting Allies in Counterinsurgency," 70.

[56]Tony Geraghty, *Inside the SAS* (New York: Ballantine, 1982), 133-134.

[57]Jeapes, *SAS: Operation Oman*, 25.

[58]CGSC Scholars Program 2010, Dhofar Veterans Panel.

[59]Geraghty, *Inside the SAS*, 135.

[60]Ladwig III, "Supporting Allies in Counterinsurgency," 72.

[61]John Townsend, Oman, 101, in *Why Insurgents Fail: Examining Post-World War II Failed Insurgencies Utilizing the Prerequisites of Successful Insurgencies as a Framework,* F. H. Zimmerman (Monterey: Naval Postgraduate School, 2007), 105.

[62]Peterson, J., *Oman's Insurgencies: The Sultanate's Struggle for Supremacy* (London: SAQI, 2007), 416.

[63]Stephen Cheney, *The Insurgency in Oman, 1962-1976* (Quantico: Marine Corps Command and Staff College, 1984), 37.

[64]Ladwig, "Supporting Allies in Counterinsurgency," 76.

[65]B. M. Niven, *Special Men and Special War–Portraits of the SAS and Dhofar* (Singapore: Imago Limited, 1990), 29.

[66]Jeapes, *SAS: Operation Oman*, 232.

[67]Ina Gardner, *In Service of the Sultan* (London: Pen and Sword, 2007).

[68]CGSC Scholars Program 2010, Dhofar Veterans Panel.

[69]John Akehurst, *We Won a War: The Campaign in Oman 1965-1975* (London: Michael Russell Publishing, 1982), 27.

[70]If the equivalent of Firqats had been created amongst the Pashtun tribesmen in the south and east Afghanistan, following the overthrow of the Taliban in 2001, and a similar civil military program had been created by an effective uncorrupted government in Kabul, perhaps the coalition would be closer to attaining its goals in Afghanistan. The Dhofar war may have been small in comparison and taken place forty years ago, but politicians and military strategists would do well to learn from this campaign.

[71]For greater understanding of America's experience in the Philippines, the author recommends: Anthony Joes, "Counterinsurgency in the Philippines" in *Counterinsurgency in Modern Warfare*, edited by Daniel Marston and Carter Malkasian. 2010, 39-49; Brian Linn, *The Philippine War, 1899-1902*, 2000, 185-224; Robert Ramsey, *Savage Wars of Peace: Case Studies of Pacification in the Philippines, 1900-1902*, Combat Studies Institute, 2007, 135-157; Alfred McCoy, *Policing America's*

Empire, 2009, 82-93; and Stanley Kornov, *In Our Image: America's Empire in the Philippines*, 1982.

[72]Khaled Musa, Deputy Chairman, Committee on Information , Moro Islamic Liberation Front (MILF), *MILF Luwaran*, 9 April 2007 (www.luwaran.com).

[73]Kilcullen, "Counterinsurgency in Iraq: Theory and Practice, 2007," Powerpoint.

[74]Statement is based on the author's firsthand experience while serving as JSOTF-P's Civil-Military Operations Chief (2008) and later as Civil Affairs Commander (2009).

[75]Department of the Army, Field Manual 3-24, 1-3.

[76]During the Philippine-American War, the US pacified the Moros through the Bates Treaty that 'officially' recognized Bangsamoro sovereignty, the first recognition of its kind which brought recognition to Moros independence.

[77]Moro people refers to a population of Muslims in the Philippines, forming the largest non-Christian group in the country, comprising about 5 percent to 10 percent of the total Philippine population. They mostly live in Mindanao and other parts of the southern Philippines.

[78]Information derived from author's grandfather, Lieutenant Colonel Vicente Figueroa, who retired from the Philippine Constabulary and actively participated in combating the Huks.

[79]CNN World, "Past war offers Afghanistan lessons. And it's not Vietnam," http://afghanistan.blogs.cnn.com/2010/01/07/past-war-offers-afghanistan-lessons-and-its-not-vietnam/ (accessed 30 November 2010).

[80]Benjamin D. Kritz, "US Policy Led to Dispute Between Muslims, Philippine Government," http://www.suite101.com/content/moro-rebellion-in-the-philippines-a63449 (accessed 10 November 2010).

[81]Michael Salman, *The Embarrassment of Slavery: Controversies over Bondage and Nationalism in the American Colonial Philippines* (Univerity of California Press, 2001), 27; and Madge Kho, "The Bates Treaty," http://www.philippineupdate.com/Bates.htm (accessed 8 October 2010).

[82]Hilario Gomez, Jr. *The Moro Rebellion and the Search for Peace: A Study on Christian-Muslim Relations in the Philippines* (Zamboanga City, Philippines: Silsilah Publications, 2000), 75.

[83]Datu Jamal Ashley Abbas, "Bangsa Moro Conflict–Historical Antecedents and Present Impact" (Speech delivered by at the University of the Philippines in Los Baños on 5 September 2000), http://jamalashley.wordpress.com/2007/04/17/bangsa-moro-conflict-historical-antecedents-and-present-impact/ (accessed 9 November 2010).

[84]Thomas M. McKenna, *Muslim Rulers and Rebels: Everyday Politics and Armed Separatism in the Southern Philippines* (Berkeley: University of California Press, 1998), 15.

[85]For additional reading on the Huk Rebellion, author recommends the following: Agoncillo, Teodoro C. (1990), *History of the Filipino People* (8th ed.); Bautista, Alberto Manuel (1952), *The Hukbalahap Movement in the Philippines, 1942-1952*; Greenburg, Lawrence M. (2010), *The Hukbalahap Insurrection: A Case Study of a Successful Anti-Insurgency Operation in the Philippines - 1946-1955;* Valeriano, Napoleon D., "Military Operations," *Counter-Guerrilla Seminar Fort Bragg, 15 June 1961.*

[86]Boyd T.Bashore, "Dual Strategy for Limited War," *Military Review* (1960), reprinted in *Modern Guerilla Warfare* by Franklin Mark Osaka, 84

[87]Kenneth M.Hammer, "Huks in the Philippines," *Military Review* (1956), reprinted in *Modern Guerilla Warfare* by Franklin Mark Osaka.

[88]Stanley Karnow, *In Our Image:America's Empire in the Philippines* (New York: Ballantine Books, 1990), 340.

[89]Daniel B. Schirmer and Stephen Rosskamm Shalom, *The Philippines Reader: A History of Colonialism, Neocolonialism, Dictatorship, and Resistance* (Cambridge, MA: South End Press, 1987), 70.

[90]Richard Kessler, *Rebellion and Repression in the Philippines* (New Haven, CT: Yale University Press, 1991), 32.

[91]Ibid.

[92]LTC Edward Geary Lansdale was a US Air Force officer who rose to the rank of Major General. He served in the Office of Strategic Services and the Central Intelligence Agency. As an early proponent of more aggressive US actions in the Cold War, Lansdale served advisor to President Magsaysay, later to President Diem, and in the early 1960s was chiefly involved in clandestine efforts to topple Fidel Castro's government.

[93]Boyd T. Bashore, "Dual Strategy for Limited War," *Military Review* (1960), reprinted in Modern Guerilla Warfare by Franklin Mark Osaka, 87

[94]Edward G. Lansdale, "Counter-Guerilla Operations in the Philippines 1946-1953" (Seminar Held at Ft. Bragg, NC, June 1961).

[95]Edwards G Lansdale, *Memorandum–Civic Activities of the Military Southeast Asia.* United States Army Special Warfare School, 1959, 2.

[96]Ibid.

[97]Ibid.

[98]Ibid., 3.

[99]Ibid., 4.

[100]Ibid.

[101]This is the author's opinion.

[102]Soliman M. Santos, Jr.,et al., *Primed and Purposeful: Armed Groups and Human Security Efforts in the Philippine. Executive Summary* (France: Natura Press, 2010), 58.

[103]Foreign internal defense is the participation by civilian and military agencies of a government in any of the action programs taken by another government or other designated organization to free and protect its society from subversion, lawlessness, and insurgency. Joint Chief of Staff, Joint Publication (JP) 3-05, *Doctrine for Joint Special Operations* (Washington, DC: Government Printing Office, 2003).

[104]Mark Bowden, "Manhunt," *The Atlantic* (March 2007), 54.

[105]Gregory Wilson, "Anatomy of Anatomy of a Successful COIN Operation: OEF-P and the Indirect Approach," *Military Review* (November-December 2006): 2.

[106]Ibid.

[107]Sepp, "Best Practices in Counterinsurgency," 8.

[108]Excerpt from JOSTF-P information video, 2009.

[109]Thom Shanker, "U.S. Counterinsurgency Unit to Stay in Philippines," *New York Times,* 20 August 2009.

[110]This was in reference to the Jolo Domestic Airport Runway improvement project completed in 2009. Although the airstrip was funded by USAID, locals make no distinction between JSOTF-P and USAID projects.

[111]The Growth in Equity III (GEM 3) is funded by the U.S. Agency for International Development and implemented in partnership with the Mindanao Economic Development Council, GEM 3 continues and expands the work carried out under GEM 1 (1995-2002) and GEM 2 (2002-2007). GEM operates throughout Mindanao, with a special focus on the Autonomous Region in Muslim Mindanao (ARMM) and other conflict-affected areas of Mindanao (CAAM).

[112]Email correspondence from a senior local government official.

[113]Ibid.

[114]Email correspondence with JSOTF-P officer.

[115]The author witnessed several ill maintained US funded town halls called area coordination centers.

[116]CGSC Scholars Progam 2010, interview with Tony Jeapes.

[117]Thomas H. Henriksen "Afghanistan, Counterinsurgency, and the Indirect Approach," JSOU Report 10-3 (Hurlburt Field, FL: Joint Special Operations University, 2010), 51-52.

[118]GEN DavidPetraeus, COMISAF Counterinsurgency Guidance Memorandum to ISAF Forces, 1 August 2010, http://www.isaf.nato.int/article/caat-anaysis-news/comisaf-coin-guidance.html (accessed 1 November 2010).

[119]GEN Stanley A. McChrystal, ISAF Commander's Counterinsurgency Guidance, http://www.isaf.nato.int/article/news/isaf-commanders-counterinsurgency-guidance.html (accessed 1 November 2010).

[120]2,403 were killed on 7 December 1941 as a result of the Japanese attack on Pearl Harbor.

[121]Jones, *Counterinsurgency in Afghanistan*, xi.

[122]International Security Assistance Force, http://www.isaf.nato.int/mission.html (accessed 20 November 2010).

[123]Ibid.

[124]Ibid.

[125]Ibid.

[126]Daniel Marston, "Realizing the Extent of Our Errors and Forging the Road Ahead," in *Counterinsurgency in Modern Warfare* eds. Daniel Marston and Carter Malkasian (Osprey Publishing, 2010), 251-285.

[127]Ibid.

[128]Anatol Lieven, "The War in Afghanistan: Its Background and Future Prospects," *Conflict, Security and Development* 9, no. 3 (October 2009), 487. Professor Anatol Lieven is Chair of International Relations and Terrorism Studies in the War Studies Department of King's College London and a Senior fellow of the New America Foundation in Washington DC.

[129]Ibid., 351-352.

[130]Egnell, "Winning Legitimacy."

[131]Ibid.

[132]Interview with SAS veterans of the Dhofar Rebellion

[133]Egnell, "Winning Legitimacy."

[134]Alexis de Tocqueville, *Democracy in America* (New York: Penguin, 1956), 103.

[135]David Kilcullen, "Counter-insurgency Redux." http://smallwarsjournal.com/documents/kilcullen1.pdf (accessed 5 November 2010), 3.

[136]Egnell, "Winning Legitimacy."

[137]Malalai Joya, *Raising My Voice: The Extraordinary Story of the Afghan Woman Who Dares to Speak Out* (London: Rider, 2009).

[138]Fitzsimmons, "Hard Hearts and Open Minds?," 358.

[139]Marston, "Realizing the Extent of Our Errors," 253.

[140]Ibid., 274.

[141]Ibid., 275.

[142]Andrea Mitchell (NBC's Chief Foreign Affairs Correspondent), "Leaked US diplomatic Cables by wikileaks.org" *NBC Nightly News*. 3 December 2010.

[143]Transparency International, "Corruption Perception Index 2010 Results," http://www.transparency.org/policy_research/surveys_indices/cpi/2010/results (accessed 1 November 2010).

[144]Octavian Manea, "Interview with Dr. David Kilcullen," *Small War Journal*, 8 November 2010, http://renekogutudartiklid.blogspot.com/2010/11/interview-with-dr-david-kilcullen.html (accessed 15 November 2010).

[145]Greg Jaffe, Scott Wilson, and Karen DeYoung, "U.S. Envoy Resists Increase in Troops," *Washington Post*, 12 November 2009.

[146]Mitchell, "Leaked US diplomatic Cables by Wikileaks.org."

[147]Andrew Wilder (Ph.D.), former Research Director at the Feinstein International Center at Tufts University and current Director for Afghanistan and Pakistan Programs, The US Institute of Peace , has led a two-year study on the assumed relationship between

foreign aid and stability in Afghanistan, Pakistan and the Horn of Africa. His team has conducted more than 400 interviews in Afghanistan trying to understand the stabilization benefits of the billions of dollars worth of development aid that have been spent so far in Afghanistan.

[148] Anna Mulrine, "A Dangerous Backslide, Age-old Problems-and a new Taliban Surge-are Dragging the Afghans Down," *US News*, 8 October 2006, http://www.usnews.com/ usnews/news/articles/061008/16afghan.htm (accessed 15 November 2010).

[149] John Heilprin, "Biden Warns of Failure in Afghanistan," *Fox News*, 25 February 2008, http://www.foxnews.com/wires/2008Feb25/0,4670,US AfghanistanBiden,00.html (accessed 16 November 2010).

[150] Andrew Wilder, "Winning Hearts and Minds?" NPR, 4 April 2010, http://npr.vo.llnwd.net/kip0/_pxn=0+_pxK=17273/anon.nprmp3/npr/me/2009/11/200911 04_me_02.mp3?dl=1 (accessed 16 November 2011).

[151] The Federally Administered Tribal Areas (FATA) are a group of small administrative units in the northwest of Pakistan, lying between the province of Khyber Pakhtunkhwa, Balochistan in the south, and the Afghanistan. They comprise seven tribal agencies and six smaller frontier regions, with considerable autonomy from the rest of Pakistan.

[152] Wilder, "Winning Hearts and Minds?"

[153] Andrew Wilder, "Weapons System Based on Wishful Thinking," *The Boston Globe,* 16 September 2009.

[154] Ibid.

[155] The Civil Operations and Revolutionary Development Support (CORDS) was formed May 1967 to coordinate the US civil and military pacification programs in Vietnam. A unique hybrid civil-military structure directly under general William C. Westmoreland, the COMUSMACV, CORDS was headed by a civilian, Ambassador Robert W. Komer, who was appointed as Westmoreland's deputy. CORDS pulled together all the various U.S. military and civilian agencies involved in the pacification effort, including the State Department, the AID, the USIA and the CIA. U.S. military or civilian province senior advisers were appointed, and CORDS civilian/military advisory teams were dispatched throughout South Vietnam's 44 provinces and 250 districts. Significant sources on CORDS include Robert Komer, *Bureaucracy at War: U.S. Performance in the Vietnam Conflict (*1986); Richard Hunt, *Pacification: The American Struggle for Vietnam's Hearts and Minds* (1995); and William Colby, *Lost Victory: A Firsthand Account of America's Sixteen-Year Involvement in Vietnam* (1990).

[156]Center for Army Lessons Learned, Handbook 09-27, *Commander's Guide to Money as a Weapon System Tactics, Techniques, and Procedures* (Fort Leavenworth, KS: Center for Army Lessons Learned April 2009), 1.

[157]U.S. Congress, House of Representatives, Hearing on U.S. Aid to Pakistan: Planning and Accountability, Committee on Oversight and Government Reform, Subcommittee on National Security and Foreign Affairs, 9 December 2009.

[158]Wilder, "Winning Hearts and Minds?," 9.

[159]Ibid.

[160]Ibid., 3.

[161]Ibid., 6.

CHAPTER 5

CONCLUSIONS AND RECOMMENDATIONS

To win the "heart," the population must believe that you have the tastiest and juiciest carrot to offer. As to "mind," they must believe that you have the biggest stick in the block, the legal mandate to use it, will to use it to protect them, and that you will be around for a good while.

— Major Winston M. Marbella

Concluding Lessons

Undoubtedly when classical counterinsurgency theorists and practitioners talk about winning a population's hearts and minds, they are not being sentimental but strategic. Influencing the "heart" means persuading the people that their interests are served best by the counterinsurgents' success while influencing the "mind" means convincing the populace that counterinsurgent forces can protect them. The population makes a cost-benefit analysis where the cost to support the insurgent is great and the benefit is minimal but the cost to support the state is low and the benefit is high. This assumes a logically thinking population and the decision based on this cost-benefit analysis, would only favor the state if the population were secure. If the cost of supporting the government is death, then most people will chose the insurgents.

The counterinsurgents of the past had a larger arsenal of coercive methods at their disposal for separating populations from insurgents. These methods might have worked for the British administration then in Malaya but are now too controversial for implementation. The tremendous leap in broadcast technology, prevalence of personal recording devices, and the internet linked global community there is not a shortage of inquisitive media. Methods that suppress human rights and violate international law will prove detrimental to any counterinsurgency campaign. A government which does not act

103

in accordance with the law forfeits the right to be called a government and cannot expect its people to obey the law.[1] The government must represent normalcy, exhibit restraint, and propagate law and order. Counterinsurgent forces represent the government to most of the people caught in the midst of war. If these forces act more irresponsibly than the guerillas themselves, the government can hardly hope to appeal to people as their protector and benefactor.[2] However, it should be noted that societies will accept coercive methods and sacrifice personal freedoms in exchange for peace and order. This was the case in Baghdad at the height of sectarian violence when T-wall barriers were erected fencing-off communities, mobility was restricted by multiple checkpoints, curfews were imposed, and vehicles, homes and personal searches were daily occurrences. In spite of all these, the population was forgiving as long as the method delivers peace and order. T-walls might be intrusive but they buy time to relocate, re-educate, and calm the passion.[3] The key is to communicate your intent and immediately ease restriction when the situation is improving.

Evidently hearts and minds has evolved from coercive heavy methods to a strategy based on winning the population's support through modernization and legitimacy. However, unlike its general acceptance in secular societies, this contemporary and very Western interpretation of modernization and legitimacy is a friction point in traditional and tribal cultures, as in the case of Afghanistan. Consideration must be given to any existing and deeply rooted socio-political framework. Accept and work through local system of authority and justice instead of infusing a new but alien Western models. You must not replace traditional legitimacy with Western efficiency.

As the first two historical case studies (Malaya and Dhofar) revealed, several counterinsurgency principles that pervade the application hearts and minds remain valid today. First and foremost, establishing security and protecting the population must be the primary concern for the counterinsurgents. Any attempts to influence a population will quickly fail if the security of the population is overlooked. Brigadier General H. R. McMaster, within the context of Iraq, states, "No amount of money or kindness, and no number of infrastructure programs, will facilitate winning over the populace if counterinsurgency forces cannot provide security to the population. Without security, nothing else matters."[4] In certain contexts, combat capability can never be replaced by soft power. If security fails it cannot be mitigated through development activities. One can only assume that the choice between supporting the international coalition and the Taliban is an easy one if it means a choice between a repressive status quo and a slight improvement in the quality of life coupled with risking your own life.

However, security by itself is not enough to make the population support the government. As written in British Army Field Manual Counterinsurgency:

> The population has to make the choice between what the insurgent offers and that which the government can provide politically, economically, and socially–the host government with it coalition partners must be seen to offer a better life. The important message that the host government should convey is that the benefits which follows once security has been restored are worth the risk, irritations, and dangers associated with the operations is necessary to achieve it.[5]

Second, only the host nation government and military can win their people's hearts and minds. The long history of counterinsurgency emphasizes that foreigners cannot win an indigenous population. It has to be local forces.[6] Galula states, "A victory is not [just] the destruction in a given area of the insurgent's forces and his political organization. It is that, plus the permanent isolation of the insurgent from the population, isolation not enforced upon the population but maintained by and with the population."[7] Key to this effort is leveraging existing sociopolitical framework instead of introducing a new system of governance. Familiarity to a system of government breeds legitimacy. This proves specially challenging to the US military in Iraq and Afghanistan. Freedom means different things to different people; democracy is not necessarily the most desirable form of governance to all. The West's attempts to impose its ideals of democracy by force of arms, therefore brought it into direct confrontation with many people in Iraq and Afghanistan. Many in Iraq, Afghanistan and the Philippines believe that the practice of their religion or role of their culture is more important than their form of political rule. Good governance comes from their religion, their family, tribal structures, and finally their traditional forms of rule, which to the West may seem autocratic but may suit them.[8]

Third, spending aid dollars for projects in order to win the population's support without conditions is an ill conceived strategy; a strategy that is based on hope and destined to fail. Identifying civil vulnerabilities with the local population's vote is important. This determines which projects are most important to the local community. However, before any project implementation takes place a dialogue must take place whereby the counterinsurgents express their expectations from the population thereby effectively leveraging the projects. But above all, the counterinsurgent must have the determination to follow through with consequences if conditions are not being met. The British SAS in Dhofar exhibited this. For instance, they would cap a well they provided if conditions and the population's behavior were not to their satisfaction. This is a powerful tool that is often missed. The lofty and misguided descriptions associated with hearts and minds, such as gentle approach, benevolence, goodwill, and kindness are attributed to the undisciplined application of stability operations projects, when, at its essence, counterinsurgency is not about happiness and goodwill or people liking us; it is about trust, confidence, and legitimacy.[9]

Fourth, heart and minds is a line of efforts and not an endstate in itself that must permeate all aspects of operation and leveraged to achieve military objectives.

Tactical Level Approach: Hearts and minds activities are primarily conducted to achieve military objectives where humanitarian assistance and development come as a secondary and tertiary effect. Although improvements in terms of humanitarian and development situations are important, they are not the main concerns of hearts and minds activities, they are humanitarian and development operations performed mainly by military units or civil-military hybrids in order to increase stability through good faith and thereby increase the legitimacy of the host nation government, as well as the international presence. The gap of discontent between the population and the government caused by unanswered civil needs is where the insurgents find ideological safe havens. It is necessary to conduct a thorough civil reconnaissance to find these gaps and prioritize the application of civic actions. Civic actions are part of stability operations distinctly different from development. For instance, the performance of MEDCAPs, VETCAPs, road construction and school renovations. Their primary objectives could be or a combination of: access to a denied population, disrupt insurgent activities or mobility, reduce insurgent effectiveness through increased HUMINT from the population, or deny safe havens. Secondary effects to these military objectives are the civil benefits of: reduced mortality rate, improved animal health, farm-to-market access, and increase literacy. As one cynical retired civil affairs officer said, "I don't like children or care for healthcare and potholes on roads outside of the US but I do have a divine purpose to build schools, conduct MEDCAPs, and build roads in distant lands - to make that S.O.B. shooting at me meet God early.[10]"

Operational Level Approach: at this level, hearts and minds is seen as a nonkinetic approach rather than a set of activities – a manner of conducting operation. It is an operational approach that is based on traditional counterinsurgency tactics of minimum force,[11] respect for and understanding of the local culture, and soft forms of force protection. The idea is that by using minimum force, being careful not to risk civilian life and property, and by generally behaving in a respectful and culturally sensitive manner, one can win the local population's hearts and minds. In connection with the wider goal, Frank Kitson noted the negative impact of excessive force, and argued that such force tends to drive the population away from the administration and towards extremist positions.[12] A Pakistani taxi driver explained it best, "If you killed my brother yesterday and today you give my village electricity, do you expect me to thank you. Would you blame me for wanting revenge?"[13]

Strategic Level Approach: The idea of winning hearts and minds refers to a way of conducting operations that will strengthen the perception of legitimacy for the host nation government, as well as for the international community presence in the country. These types of activities generally involve specialized units in information operations (IO), public affairs operations (PAO), and military information support operations (MISO) in an attempt to influence the local population.[14] As the main objective is not to achieve development per se, each project must be communicated for maximum impact.

108

The strategic feature of narratives lies in the fact that they are not spontaneous, but "deliberately constructed or reinforced out of the ideas and thoughts that are already current."[15] Smith argues that in the struggle for the hearts and minds of the local population, the number of battlefield victories or reconstruction projects completed matter little if the population thinks you are not winning, or visibly improving people's situations. Instead, the achievement of victory takes place by communicating with the people through the media and other outlets, getting the right narrative out there and changing perceptions.[16] For instance, if you built a hospital in Town "A" but failed to spread the word to the people in Town "B," then to the Town B folks the hospital never happened. A prime IO opportunity here is missed. It is impossible to change people's perceptions if positive actions are not being communicated. It is not enough for the government to do and be good; to be persuasive, it has to also appear good in the minds of the people.[17]

Recommendations

This thesis offers two recommendations for immediate consideration by current counterinsurgency practitioners in the field - review the manner development-aid dollars are allocated and the value of religion as a critical avenue of influence.

Development-Aid Accountability

As previously discussed in the Afghan case study, the manner development-aid dollars are applied in Afghanistan is falling short of expectations, fueling corruption, and could be funding the Taliban. One research suggests that ISAF is failing to win Afghan hearts and minds not because we have spent too little money, but because we have spent too much too quickly, often in insecure environments with extremely limited implementation and oversight capacity.[18] According to a recently returned US Army brigade commander:

> There are a lot of bilateral donors but efforts and resources must come in at a central point for appropriate distribution. We are moving at the speed of war but the local governments cannot move as fast as coalition effort due to lack of host nation agencies capacity and the education of local leaders.[19]

The Afghan local governments do not have systems in place or the capacity to effectively absorb and account for the huge windfall of development-aid dollars. Three-time Pulitzer Prize winner Thomas Friedman in his book *The Lexus and the Olive Tree* compares countries to the parts of a computer; the hardware, the operating system, and the software.[20] He defines hardware as "the basic shell around your economy," and says that throughout the cold war there were three kinds of hardware in the world: free-market capitalist, communist, and hybrid hardware that combined the first two.[21] The operating system is the broad macro-economic policy of the country, and the software is the legal and regulatory systems of the country. Compared with Afghanistan, the country might now have an evolving hybrid hardware (economy) and operating system (macro-economic policy) but lacks the appropriate software (regulatory systems) to handle the huge influx of development dollars.

The solution is not to stop spending but rather continuing investment on development objectives only to the point it can be accounted for. The quantity of projects built must not be the basis for success. Alternatively, it is the project's quality and effectiveness in changing local behaviors that must be given emphasis. A US Civil Affairs battalion commander said it best:

The insurgency exists not because there are issues with public utilities. There is a [government] moral legitimacy problem, not issues with public services. The insurgents have more influence and legitimacy than the government. They are ruthless, but that only carries them so far. Spending money does not solve the problem. This is not the way to approach insurgency. Money is a tool not a solution. Also, you can't fix everything for host nation. We can enable them but not do it for them. There has to be pre-conditions to use of funds.[22]

Of equal importance to identifying civil vulnerabilities (needs) and nominating projects for funding, the capacity of the local government must be assessed. Can they manage and maintain the project and have the means to account every dollar spent? Failure to do so causes a vicious cycle of funding insecurity by throwing money at the places with the least ability to spend it well. Wilder explains:

We have to recognize that political legitimacy in Afghanistan hasn't historically been based on providing services, but on protection and justice. One way to help improve the government is to focus on the appointments mechanisms. Good individuals can change the face of a ministry. In fact, in the cases when a development project was viewed favorably, the credit was usually given to the individual in charge.[23]

Of equal importance to accountability is building the local government's capacity and the avoidance of imposing Western systems of governance and processes. This is always a factor when dealing with foreign populations. Counterinsurgents must respect and work within the existing social and political framework, even if it is inefficient and counter-intuitive to proven Western practice and mindset; it must be allowed the opportunity to work. A system that is widely accepted and been exiting for centuries has its merits. It has legitimacy in the local populations. Do not parallel foreign systems to Western efficiency. Allowing the local process to work builds the host nation's capacity which in the long run is more desirable than current results. This calls for tactical patience and could prove challenging to the military whose culture is based on results and efficiency, coupled with the approaching 2014 troop withdrawal deadline.

Over the years, and by necessity, military personnel made strides in understanding development and have ventured deeper into this realm. This could be attributed to two factors. First is the current evolving doctrine that has full spectrum operations anchored on "stability operations." Second the huge influx of development dollars to be leveraged for military objectives as evident by the Money as a Weapon System has forced the military to take on developmental projects which are normally in the province of USAID and other nongovernmental organizations (NGOs). The military's involvement in these projects can enhance the image of the US military and create a bridge with the civil society. However, the military's effective involvement in longer term institution-building could be inhibited. Secretary Robert Gates had raised serious doubts about the merit of these operations becoming a military mission.[24] Conventional soldiers are not trained to work with foreign cultures, languages, and civil communities. Even the US Army's Civil Affairs Branch whose Soldiers' core task involves support to civil administration have limited knowledge on long term development. The military's contribution to development must be limited to providing security, assisting relief efforts, and infrastructure reconstruction when these activities are rationalized part of the immediate security mission.

Winning Hearts and Souls

Religion, specifically Islam, is one of the strongest determinants in both the life of the community and the life of the individual in the conflict areas where US military is currently engaged (Iraq, Afghanistan, southern Philippines, and the Horn of Africa). Hearts and minds are most strongly affected by religious beliefs. Islam has long been, and continues to be a force that rules the lives of people in these areas. It is a powerful force of influence, able to mobilize masses, and in winning hearts and minds. Yet, in the US foreign policy culture over the past decades, government structures continue to consider religion a dangerously sensitive area and allocate minimal resource to leverage religion in foreign cultures.[25] According Mohammad Sediq Chakari, "It is only by engaging the religious community that we will be able to fight extremist ideology. The international community has so far ignored the clergy."[26] The US government's failure to take seriously religious motivations for public human behavior, at least as seriously as we do the incentives of power, politics and material gain, has placed the security of the American people at risk.[27] This was apparent throughout the oral history interviews conducted for this paper.

When asked about leveraging religion to influence foreign populations, all the American respondents offered a resounding aversion towards the idea. When asked about applying aid dollars in mosque or Islamic activities, a former ambassador expressed:

> All religions present problems. It ties up CA operations. If you want to fix in the mosque, fix the part which is a school, or call it an education center, fix that. Stay away from religion. It ties up funds.[28]

On the contrary, a great majority of senior British military officers approves the method and see its benefits. One general officer remarked, "Religion is an angle the UK is struggling with like the US. The Afghans themselves thinks that religion is a good angle for engagement."[29] Another senior British officer went further with, "The religious aspect bridges multiple divides that ISAF has failed to bridge. However, policy makers see support of Islam as undermining the campaign." When asked about employing money to leverage religion, he stated, "UK money can be used for Muslim related activities."[30] While mentioned earlier in the Philippine case study, JSOTF-P is prohibited from engaging religious structures and activities unless to repair damages caused by counterinsurgent forces.

Similar to the Anglo-American divide on heart and minds' understanding, religion is sticking point. Could this be due to the British vast colonization experiences of multiple cultures as oppose to America's limited exposure? In Dhofar, British SAS veterans expressed, "[we] built mosque at every government center along with a clinic, school, shops, and a well." A definite contributor to America's fiscal aversion towards religion is rooted in its strong sense of separation of church and government; the attitude that any use of religion by the government is a violation of the first amendment.[31] This attitude is a deeply entrenched American dogma and permeates in its application of US dollars in influencing foreign populations. The American lack of acknowledgement and understanding of religion's relevance domestically contributes to its failure to recognize religions importance abroad. It fails to grasp that it is a powerful motivating factor in foreign politics and populations. America's religious neutrality should not preclude it from leveraging religion in Muslim nations with populations who do not differentiate or abide by the Western concept of church and government separation. Indeed, they find it incomprehendable. The most critical aspect of American disposition towards non-Western societies is the pronounced inability or unwillingness to come to terms with religion, philosophies, ideology, and other bodies of beliefs that have decisively shaped the foreign mind-set but which continue to baffle Americans."[32]

Religion, specifically Islam, is a fundamental pillar and a defining characteristic of the populations where US forces are currently deployed (e.g. Iraq, Afghanistan, and the southern Philippines). It is a potent source of influence that deeply permeates their social fabric. The insurgents, with their keen understanding of this fact, are quick and masterful in leveraging religion to their advantage and placing the coalition in a negative light. Religion is an area where coalition forces have allocated minimal resources and attention while insurgents continue to dominate. In an Islamic society that does not delineate between politics and religion, winning the 'hearts and souls' is fundamentally a religious issue. By not actively allocating resources in the religious realm, the coalition is playing into the insurgent hands and missing the mark.

A significant part of the Taliban's narrative proclaims that GIRoA is a puppet government, allowing infidel foreign troops to kill and harass ordinary Muslims because of their religious identity. This portrayal erodes GIRoA's legitimacy and emasculates it in its people's eyes. It depicts the government as powerless as its Muslim citizens are victimized and exploited by an occupying force. A delicate approach must be taken to solicit a credible voice that would counter such narrative, and this voice can only come from empowered Afghan religious leaders. Perhaps worth considering are the following strategies:

1. The current lack of educational facilities and affordable access for religious students drives many across the border towards Pakistan. Insurgents gain access to them and corrupt their view of the world through radical Islamic indoctrination. By not investing monies to correct this distorted path to Islamic education, opportunity is lost to influence young minds and the future of peaceful Islam in Afghanistan is bankrupt. The country needs more dynamic and secular religious leaders to engage the largely young population. By investing in Madaris and secular Mosque schools, the foundation is laid to a

115

much peaceful future. However, as a word of caution, religious figures are but one set of actors in a field of multiple power brokers that holds a community together. It is important to realize that they are not the elixir or a cure-all for the winning hearts and souls. Although severely lacking at this time, the coalition must temper its support to religious leaders and balance this with empowering local elders as well. The coalition must hedge its bets due to changing tide of communal power. A balance between Islam and Pashtuwali must be taken into consideration.

2. Leverage relations with trusted local mullahs to issue anti-insurgent fatwas. A fatwa is an Islamic religious ruling, a scholarly opinion on a matter of Islamic law. A fatwa is issued by a recognized religious authority in Islam. But since there is no hierarchical priesthood or anything of the sort in Islam, a fatwa is not necessarily "binding" on the faithful. The people who pronounce these rulings are supposed to be knowledgeable, and base their rulings in knowledge and wisdom. They need to supply the evidence from Islamic sources for their opinions, and it is not uncommon for scholars to come to different conclusions regarding the same issue.[33]

3. Leverage the concept of 'Isaal al-Thawab' to assist in counterinsurgency operations--an Islamic belief of accruing rewards for doing good deeds or activities for the sake of Allah. Women in particular are keen to perform acts which bring thawab. The key to thawab are the mullahs. They identify and provide guidance to which acts earn thawab and which ones do not. This is a powerful concept which has significant influence potential. If leveraged

116

appropriately a cooperative mullah may declare that reporting IED sites, IED factory locations, and IED makers earns thawab as it saves lives of innocent Muslim civilians and killing fellow Muslims is against Islamic teachings. This powerful message could be further amplified if disseminated through different media with a text-in number for reporting.

4. Another concept for consideration is the significance of the hajj. It is the fifth pillar of Islam, a religious duty that must be carried out at least once in their lifetime by every able-bodied Muslim who can afford to do so. This could be leveraged to compliment the Rewards for Justice Program (RFJ).[34] Evidently, not all individuals are motivated by money and perhaps a theological incentive could be a stronger lure. Consider adding a guaranteed Hajj visit to Mecca for the informer and all immediate family members. This provides a means to fulfill an Islamic duty.

5. Lastly, reverse the Taliban's banning of multiple Afghan religious festivals that were declared un-Islamic. Encourage Afghans to celebrate these again. By doing so, secularism is encouraged, pre-Taliban normalcy is established, and open public defiance of the Taliban is demonstrated. For instance, the Naw Ruz (New Year's Day) which was originally a pagan spring equinox festival assimilated by Islam from its arrival in Iran and Afghanistan over a thousand years ago. This or other celebrations could further be leveraged to remind Afghans, most especially the youth, the link of Islam and prosperity – a celebration of Islam's tolerance and progressiveness in science, arts, literature etc. While a majority of the Islamic world cherishes Islam's Golden Age,[35] this

runs contradictory to the Taliban's intent to throw Afghanistan back in the Stone Age. This should encourage the youth to reach out to the global community, aspire for a better future and embrace modernity since Islam once led world innovation.

Beyond Basic Culture

In addition to religion, cultural norms must be considered for leverage as well. Current counterinsurgency practitioners understand the significance of foreign cultures; this understanding must extend beyond the customary study of elementary customs, courtesies, and basic phrases. Counterinsurgents must learn how to use deeply rooted cultural norms and ethnic intricacies in order influence hearts and minds.

An extreme case was the experience and survival of PO1 Marcus Luttrell. He was the lone survivor of his 4-man SEAL Team 10 that was engaged by an overwhelming number of Taliban fighters in Afghanistan. Badly wounded, he managed to walk and crawl seven miles. He was given shelter by tribesmen from Sabri-Minah, a Pashtun village. This was done because of "Lokhay Warkawa," a Pashtunwali[36] belief that any stranger in need of shelter must be given it.[37] The villagers sheltered him and provided medical aid, and refused Taliban demands that Luttrell be turned over to them. After several days one of the village elders trekked twenty miles to a US base to reveal Luttrell's location, and he was finally rescued six days after the battle by US forces. When asked about this Pashtunwali custom, Luttrell replied, "once they offer you assistance or I ask for assistance, then its 2000 years of custom that they are honor bound to protect me."[38]

Luttrell's case merits a deeper examination in the relationship (or contradiction) between Islam and Pashtunwali. Is Pashtunwali deeper embedded in the Pastuns' consciousness than Islam? Evidently these Pashtun tribesmen risk everything by going against the Taliban which promulgates an ultra-conservative form of Islam. As such, should counterinsurgents' emphasis on religious leaders shift to village elders in Afghanistan? Is it Pashtunwali or Islam that truly dominates the Pashtuns' hearts and minds?

Final Thoughts

Hearts and minds played a critical role in the past and continue to influence current counterinsurgency campaigns. However, this thesis illuminated the terms complexity and lingering controversies since its inception in the Malayan Emergency. In its most simplistic explanation, to win the emotive 'heart' the population must believe that you have the tastiest and juiciest carrot to offer while to win the cognitive 'mind', the population must believe that you have the biggest stick in the block, the legal mandate to use it, will to use it to protect them, and that you will be around for a good while. However, as Clausewitz stated, "Everything in war is very simple but the simplest thing is difficult."

The challenge to understand hearts and minds is complex. It is only surpassed by the greater challenges of its effective implementation and the creation of a metric to gauge its effectiveness. It demands tremendous intellectual capacity and historical understanding. Perhaps winning hearts and minds is misleading. How does one measure winning the population's hearts and minds? What you are really trying to do is bring them over to your side of the middle. Not all the way over, but just enough. At times keeping the population on the fence and not aiding the insurgents is sufficient.

The term's inception is mired with controversy and Malaya will continue to be a hotbed for debate. Nonetheless, the successful but coercive hearts and minds methods applied then will be difficult to conceal or justify in today's technology connected world. Its current manifestation and application through Western interpretation of modernization and legitimacy is challenged in non-secular cultures. Perhaps a better alternative to winning hearts and minds is providing local populations clarity of choice and certainty of future. This entails a clear choice that siding with counterinsurgents guarantees safety and an improved standard of living; and that the preservation of cultures, religion, and local values are certain.

Considering all that has been said, hearts and minds will remain as a bumper sticker. Its complexity and associated historical baggage will preclude most counterinsurgency practitioners in effectively grasping this concept in the manner that it should be understood. It will continue to suggest niceness and begs the question, "Why don't they (population) like us?" The fact of the matter is that they do not need to love Americans. US soldiers should not be the first in the picture. It should be the host nation for only the host nation's forces can win their population. Perhaps hearts and minds should be left where it is at – in history's dustbin.

---

[1]Robert Thompson, *Defeating Communist Insurgency* (London: Praeger, Publishers, 1966), 52.

[2]Statement of Che Guevara, quoted in Paret and Shy, "Guerilla Warfare and US Military Policy: A Study" in *The Guerilla and How to Fight Him* ed. T. N. Greene (New York: Praeger, 1962), 51.

[3]CGSC Scholars Progam 2010, AA505.

[4]H. R. McMaster cited in Chris Gibson, "Battlefield Victories and Strategic Success: The Path Forward in Iraq," *Military Review* (September-October 2006).

[5]British Army, British Army Field Manual, *Counterinsurgenct*, Volume 1 Part 10 January 2010, 3-9

[6]Manea, "Interview with Dr. David Kilcullen."

[7]David Galula cited in, *South-east Asian Spectrum*, Volumes 1-3, University of Michigan, 1972, 34.

[8]Ibid.

[9]CGSC Scholars Progam 2010, AA505.

[10]Confidential conversation with retired a Civil Affairs officer.

[11]Minimum Force--Those minimum actions, including the use of armed force, sufficient to bring a situation under control or to defend against hostile act or hostile intent. All actions must cease as soon as the target complies with instructions or ceases hostile action. The firing of weapons is to be considered as a means of last resort. Joint Chiefs of Staff, Joint Publication (JP) 1-02*, Department of Defense Dictionary of Military and Associated Terms* (Washington, DC: Department of Defense, 2005),.344.)

[12]CGSC Scholars Progam 2010, AA1009.

[13] CGSC Scholars Program 2010, Dhofar Veterans Panel.

[14]Ministry of Defense, Joint Warfare Publication (JWP) 3-50, *Military Contributions to Peace Support Operations* (DSDA Operations Centre, 2004), D-24.

[15]Lawrence Freedman, *The Transformation of Strategic Affairs* (London: Routledge, 2006), 22.

[16]Rupert Smith, *The Utility of Force: The Art of War in the Modern World*, New York: Knopf, 2007, 391.

[17]Riley Sunderland, *Wining the Hearts and Minds of the People: Malaya, 1948-1960* (Santa Monica, CA: RAND Corp, 1964), 28.

[18]Andrew Wilder, "Weapons System' Based on Wishful Thinking," *Boston Globe*, 16 September 2009.

[19]CGSC Scholars Progam 2010, AA618

[20]Thomas Friedman, *The Lexus and the Olive Tree, Understanding Globalization* (New York: Anchor Books, 2000).

[21]Ibid.

[22]CGSC Scholars Progam 2010, AA601

[23]Wilder, "Winning Heart and Minds?"

[24]J. Brian Atwood, "Elevating Development Assistance," *Prism* 1, no.3, http://www.ndu.edu/press/elevating-development-assistance.html (accessed 17 November 2010).

[25]Jennifer A. Marshall, "Mediators of the Message: The Role of Religion and Civil Society in Public Diplomacy." in *Strategic Influence – Public Diplomacy, Counterpropaganda and Political Warfare,* ed. J. Michael Waller (Washington, DC: Institute of World Politics Press, 2009), 101.

[26]Isobel Coleman and Masuda Sultan, "Afghan Mullahs Key To American Success: Analysis," *Huffington Post,* 17 July 2009.

[27]Thomas F. Farr, Director, Office of International Religious Freedom, State Department Office, cited by Jennifer A. Marshall, "Effective Ideological Engagement Requires Understanding of Religion." in *Strategic Influence – Public Diplomacy, Counterpropaganda and Political Warfare,* ed. J. Michael Waller, 232.

[28]CGSC Scholars Progam 2010, AA801.

[29]CGSC Scholars Progam 2010, AA1011.

[30]Ibid.

[31]The Establishment Clause of the First Amendment prohibits the establishment of a national religion by the Congress or the preference of one religion over another, non-religion over religion, or religion over non-religion.

[32]Adda B. Bozeman, "Knowledge and Method in Comparative Intelligence Studies," in *Strategic Influence & Statecraft* (Washington, DC: Brassey, 1992), 191.

[33]Muslims look at the reputation of the person giving it, the evidence given to support the fatwa, and then decide whether to follow it or not. When there are conflicting opinions issued by different scholars, they compare the evidence and then choose the opinion to which their conscience dictates.

[34]Rewards for Justice (RFJ) is the counterterrorism rewards program of the U.S. Department of State's Diplomatic Security Service (DSS). The Secretary of State is currently offering rewards for information that prevents or favorably resolves acts of

international terrorism against U.S. persons or property worldwide. For instance, Mullah Omars commands a $10M rewards for information leading to his capture.

[35]The Islamic Golden Age is traditionally dated from the mid-8th century to the mid-13th century A.D. (sack of Baghdad by Hulagu, the grand-son of Gengis-Khan).

[36]Pashtunawali is an ancient feudal tribal "code of honor," that predates Islam. It is an unwritten, democratic, socio-political culture, law and ideology of the Pashtun society inherited from their forefathers and carried on to the present generation. It is a dominant force of Pashtun culture and identity.

[37]"A Former Navy SEAL Questions Rules of War," *Morning Edition* (NPR), 13 August 2007, http://www.npr.org/templates/story/story.php?storyId=12690379 (accessed 5 November 2010).

[38]"Interview with Matt Lauer," *Today Show*, 12 June 2007, http://www.msnbc.msn.com/id/19189482/ (accessed 5 November 2010).

APPENDIX A

CGSC SCHOLARS PILOT PROGRAM INFORMATION PAPER

INFORMATION PAPER

10-02 SG 1E   28 July 2010

SUBJECT: Command and General Staff College (CGSC) Scholars Program 2010 (Pilot)

General: The 21st century security environment is one of complexity and uncertainty. The United States Army CGSC has determined that the current program of Intermediate Level Education (ILE) provided to field grade officers may not be sufficient for educating our future leaders for the complex challenges of this environment. Therefore, the CGSC Commandant, at the advice and direction of the Chief of Staff of the Army, created the CGSC Scholar's Program.

Concept: Students selected for the Scholars Research Program are assigned to a seminar group. Each seminar is organized around a research topic of interest. Some examples of these topics may include "Modern Applications of Human Intelligence" or "Facing Asymmetric Threats". Upon successfully completing the CGSC Scholars Program, students receive an MMAS degree.

Selection: In order to participate in the program, CGSC students (O-4 to O-5) volunteer to compete in a selection process that considers past operational experience, educational background, interest in joining an enhanced educational program, and potential contributions to the seminar. CGSC Scholars complete all Core Curriculum requirements for the Intermediate Level Education (ILE) before starting the research seminar.

Faculty: Dr. Daniel Marston, Ike Skelton Chair in Counterinsurgency and renowned historian, serves as the faculty lead for the first CGSC Scholars Pilot. Other members of the faculty team come from the Department of Command and Leadership, Department of History, with research faculty. All CGSC Scholars faculty have a terminal academic degree.

Program: The initial Pilot (class 10-02) has four Lines of Instruction. The initial main effort and overall seminar theme focused on History of Counterinsurgency. Curriculum dealt with eight insurgency case studies that included Northern Ireland, Rhodesia, Malaya, Vietnam, Iraq, and Afghanistan. The Leadership and History lines covered material similar to existing CGSC lessons. Research lessons covered basic methods, advanced qualitative research methods, and a thesis seminar.

Schedule: The initial CGSC Scholars Program had three major phases. In Phase 1 (Academics) Leadership, History, and Research meet for four hours one day over nine weeks. The COIN sessions meets for four hours, twice each week. In Phase 2 (Implementation), students conduct field research for approximately seven weeks and then devote around four weeks to writing an MMAS thesis. In Phase 3 (Closeout) students have about ten days to provide briefings on their research, conduct their AAR, and prepare for CGSC graduation.

Research: CGSC Scholars conduct primary source research. This research may involve travel around the country, to allied nations, and when possible, directly into a theater of operations. Students conduct field research with practitioners, senior leaders, and policy makers. This research often includes oral history interviews as well as collection of relevant data at each location.

Bottom Line: The CGSC Scholars program is an intense, "accelerated" educational experience that provides graduates with tools to meet challenges through Senior Level Education.

POC: Dr. Daniel Marston, 913-684-4567, daniel.p.marston@us.army.mil. Dr. Clark, 913-684-4752, thomas.clark19@us.army.mil.

APPENDIX B

INTERVIEW QUESTIONS

A. Pre-Deployment Preparations
1. Describe your organization's mission and how it fit into the counterinsurgency effort. (Ken)
2. What did you and your unit do to prepare for deployment? (Carrie)
3. Describe how you used COIN manuals? (Carrie)

B. Relations with other US Agencies
1. How would you define the command relationship between your unit or parent unit and other US agencies? Describe the relationship? (May prompt, PRT, DOS, USAID, CIA etc) (Ken)
2. Describe your unit's relationship with SOF. (Ken/Jesse)
3. How did JSOA/ROZ affected both SOF and conventional forces? (Jesse)
4. How do you view the role of SOF in COIN campaigns? (Jesse)

C. Relations with Host Nation/ Security Forces Interaction
1. Describe your relationship with host nation security forces (national, regional, and local) and how did you integrate them. (Ken/Carrie)
2. How did your unit or your parent unit coordinate efforts with the host nation government (national, district and or local)? (Ken)
3. How effective was your interaction host nation government, local authorities, and local security forces? (Carrie)
4. Describe specific instances of corruption, how can you mitigate corrupt host nation officials, and what measure have you witnessed at vetting or screening to ensure host nation forces are not infiltrated by insurgents? (Travis)
5. How did you task organize your unit in order to "partner" with host nation security forces? (Mac)
6. Describe the command relationship between the security forces you worked with and the host nation government (nation, district, and local)? (Ken)
7. Did you conduct any special training or education to prepare the Soldiers that would be working with indigenous forces for that assignment? (Mac)
8. Did your preparations/training make your unit better able to employ local security forces? (Carrie)

D. COIN Actions

1. Describe the in-theater training process your unit went though? (Mac)
2. As to Heart and Minds, what did you do to win or control the population? (Matt)
3. Describe how development dollars affected the population's behavior and was a dialogue held with local leaders IOT leverage these projects to achieve US/Host Nation objectives? (Matt)
4. Describe how you used PSYOP (MISO) and IO in your operations? (Travis)
5. Have you witnessed any cases of military deception MILDEC? (Travis)
6. How did your unit convey your narrative (define) to the population IOT gain their support? (Karsten)
7. As to population and resource control, how did you secure or separate the local population from insurgents? (Matt)
8. Did the operational boundaries of your unit or parent unit match the civil boundaries (district, village, city)? (Ken)
9. Did a plan, operation, action, activity, or initiative ever have unintentional positive outcome? (Mike)
10. Was there an amnesty program in your AOR? Describe it? If not, did you observe opportunities for reintegration and reconciliation? (Karsten)
11. Describe the use of turned or flipped insurgents in COIN (use of former insurgents groups to work for the government through incentives)? (Travis)
12. Based on your experience, what do you think amnesty, reconciliation and reintegration should be? What should its end effect be? (Karsten)

E. Lessons Learned

1. Did you do something that was not based in doctrine that had positive results? (Mike/ Carrie)
2. Looking back at the whole deployment, did you ever do something that disrupted, reduced, or nullified insurgent intelligence collection, information operations, C2, fire and maneuver, or leadership? (Mike)
3. What did you feel was the most effective part of countering the insurgency and can you provide any examples that you witnessed? (Karsten)
4. How would you use combat tracking in COIN? (Travis)
5. What would you do differently for your next deployment? And any final comments? (Carrie)

CONSOLIDATED COIN THEMES:

Are there historic lessons from counterinsurgency campaigns with respect to counterinsurgent organizational models that facilitated unity of command or effort and positive effects that could be applied or adapted for current or future counterinsurgency campaigns? (Ken)

How can counterinsurgency be employed through the use of local security forces and further supported by both pre-conflict and later-developed versions of doctrine? (Carrie)

How can government forces turn insurgents for pseudo operations and use them to find and destroy other insurgents?(Travis)

Can counterinsurgency be conducted more effectively at the tactical level by taking away or undermining the strengths of the insurgent force in regards to the Elements of Combat Power?(Mike)

Could previously successful hearts and minds strategies be applied to current day population and resource control (PRC) methods in conducting counterinsurgency? (Matt)

How has the United States Special Operation Forces (often looked upon by the rest of the Army to lead in institutional change) evolved in counterinsurgency conflicts in the past century, mainly from lessons learned of counterinsurgencies such as Malaya (British SAS), Vietnam (American Special Forces) and Dhofar (British SAS)? (Jesse)

How have we as militaries in the United States and Great Britain planned for counterinsurgency operations and subsequently trained and organized our forces to implement them? (Mac)

How does the strategy and tactic of amnesty for enemies affect past insurgencies and their counter insurgency effort? (Karsten)

APPENDIX C

INFORMED CONSENT FORM

INTRODUCTION

You are invited to participate in a research study exploring counterinsurgency (COIN) from both a scholars' and a practitioners' perspective. You were chosen based upon the simple criteria that you have served in some capacity, either military or civilian, in a counterinsurgency effort.

This study is being conducted as primary source research to support the efforts of the Command and General Staff College Scholars Program and the researchers' completion of theses for Master of Military Art and Science degrees. CGSC students (O-4 to O-5) have volunteered to compete in a selection process that considered past operational experience, educational background, interest in joining an enhanced educational program, and potential contributions to the seminar. CGSC Scholars completed all Core Curriculum requirements for the Intermediate Level Education (ILE) before starting the research seminar.

This interview is being conducted in accordance with US Army Center for Military History guidelines. Interviews are solely for the purpose of oral history.

RESEARCH PURPOSE

The purpose of this study is to define COIN from both a literature and a practitioner's point of view. Literature reviewed by the researchers includes original doctrine, case studies, and classicists' perspectives. Practitioners can provide aspects of their personal experience that will further help to define COIN. Both literature and shared information will be analyzed and compared, with appropriate citations provided.

Ultimately, the ILE Scholars will publish their findings as theses for a Masters in Military Arts and Science for the military's wider use. Your participation will significantly assist in this goal.

RESEARCH PROCEDURES

If you agree to participate in this study, I would ask you to participate in an interview and potentially be available for follow-up clarification. The interview will last between one to two hours, and the topics discussed will include themes surrounding COIN. The purpose of the interview will not only address specified questions, but also your personal experiences and perspectives on COIN. You will be free to decline to answer any question. The interview will be recorded to assure accurate transcription of your perspectives. You may decline to be recorded or stop the recording while the interview is in progress.

Because the interview will be shared with eight members of the Scholars Program and their faculty advisors, additional clarification may be requested by one of the researchers. If you agree, you will be asked for contact information (email address, phone number) so you can be reached. Any further contact will follow the same rules of confidentiality as agreed upon before, and will be reviewed prior to any additional contact.

CONFIDENTIALITY

There is some choice regarding the level of confidentiality that will be ensured for this study. Given the high-profile nature of the potential participants, I ask that you choose whether and to what extent you may be identified. There are three possible levels:

_____ No Personal Attribution. Names and organizations of those interviewed *will not be published*. Only contextual criteria will be included for clarity of information (e.g., Commanding Officer of an Armor Brigade; company-grade staff officer for a battalion-sized element). The participant's name and affiliation *will not used on audio files or transcripts* (if identification is made by mistake, it will be deleted from the transcript. Data provided will be identified by a code number. Any quotes or interview excerpts *will not be attributed* to the participant by name or in any way that could lead to identification of the participant. Your unit will not specifically be mentioned. Your tenure in theater may be alluded to in order to provide context (e.g., This officer served in both the early phases of Operation Iraqi Freedom and a mature theater in Operation Enduring Freedom.). For clarity, years may be used. Please provide a future date when this restriction can be upgraded:

_____ Partial Personal Attribution. Names and organizations of those interviewed *will be published*. Quotes/excerpts will not be accompanied with a name or information that could lead to identification. Data provided will be identified by a code number. Names or specific affiliations will not be included in any report or publication of the study findings. Please provide a future date when this restriction can be upgraded:

_____ Full Personal Attribution. Names and organizations of those interviewed *will be published* and *quotes will be attributed* to the participant personally, by name and by organization.

Please review the three potential levels of confidentiality and disclosure, and choose one by marking your initials on the blank to the left of the choice you prefer.

In addition, to protect the confidentiality of participants of this study, the master list of names, audio recordings, transcriptions, and notes will be property of the United Stated Government and will reside with the Ike Skelton Chair for Counterinsurgency (Dr. Daniel Marston, please see below for contact information) the Command and General Staff College, Fort Leavenworth, KS under appropriate US Army Regulations and Policies.

VOLUNTARY NATURE OF THE STUDY

Taking part in this research study is completely voluntary. Your decision whether or not to participate in this study will not affect your current or future relations with the Command and General Staff College. If you decide to participate, you are free to withdraw at any time.

For your protection, you have the right to request that the researchers stop the recording device, discontinue taking notes, etc. Information you provide "off the record" will not be used as quotations in a thesis, but may provide context and/or background for certain topics.

SECURITY

Interviews will be conducted at the UNCLASSIFIED level.

HOW TO GET ANSWERS TO YOUR QUESTIONS

You are encouraged to ask questions both before you agree to be in this study and also at any time you need information in the future. Dr. Daniel Marston holds the Ike Skelton Chair for Counterinsurgency at the Command and General Staff College and exercises faculty oversight for this research project. You may contact him directly at any time. He can be reached at daniel.marston@balliol-oxford.com or daniel.p.marston@us.army.mil. Alternately, please call him with questions at (913) 684-4567.

You may also contact Dr. Robert Baumann, Director of the Command and General Staff Graduate Degree program. He can be reached at robert.f.baumann@us.army.mil or by phone at (913) 684-2752.

STATEMENT OF CONSENT

I have read the above information. I have asked questions and received answers. I consent to participate in this study.

I will be given a copy of this form for my records.

_____

Signature   Date

I have fully explained this research study to the participants, and in my judgment, there was sufficient information regarding risks and benefits, to enable the participant make an informed decision. I will inform the participant in a timely manner of any changes in the procedure or risks and benefits if any should occur.

_____

Signature   Date

BIBLIOGRAPHY

Books

Ahlstrom, Sydney E,. and David D. Hall. *A Religious History of the American People.* New Haven CT: Yale University Press, 2004.

Akehurst, John. *We Won a War: The Campaign in Oman 1965-1975.* London: Michael Russel Publishing, 1982.

Allen, Charles. *The Savage Wars of Peace: Soldier's Voices 1945-1989.* London: Michael Joseph Publishing, 1990.

Anderson, David. *Histories of the Hanged: Britain's Dirty War in Kenya and the End of Empire.* London: Phoenix, 2005.

Andrade, Dale. *Westmoreland was right: Learning the wrong lessons from the Vietnam War.* Small Wars and Insurgencies, June 2008.

Beckett, Ian. "The British Counter-insurgency Campaign in Dhofar, 1965-1975." In *Counterinsurgency in Modern Warfare,* by Daniel and Carter Malkasian Marston, Ian Beckett, "The British Counter-insurgency Campaign in Dhofar, 1965-1975," in Daniel Marston and Carter175-190. Oxford: Osprey Publishing, 2010.

Bedlington, Stanley. *Malaysia and Singapore: The Building of New States.* Ithaca: Cornell University Press, 1978.

Bergerud, Eric. *The Dynamics of Defeat: The Vietnam War in Hau Nghia Province.* Oxford: Westview Press, 1991.

Bogart, Adrian. *One Valley at a Time.* JSOU Report 06-6, Hurlburt Field, FL: Joint Special Operations University, August 2006.

Bremer, L. Paul. *My Year in Iraq.* New York: Simon & Schuster, 2006.

Campbell, Kurt M., and Richard Weitz. *Non-Military Strategies For Countering Islamist Terrorism: Lessons Learned From Past Counterinsurgecies.* The Princeton Project Papers, Princeton, NJ: Princeton University, 2007.

Cheney, Stephen. *The Insurgency in Oman, 1962-1976.* Quantico: Marine Corps Command and Staff College, 1984.

Clausewitz, Carl von. *On War.* Edited and translated by Michael Howard and Peter Paret. Princeton, NJ: Princeton University Press, 1976.

Cloake, John. *Templer: Tiger of Malaya: The Life of Field Marshall Sir Gerald Templer.* London: Harrap Publishing, 1985.

Clutterbuck, Richard L. *The Long, Long War: Counterinsurgency in Malaya and Vietnam*. New York: Frederick A. Praeger, 1966.

Coates, John. *Suppressing Insurgency*. Boulder, CO: Westview Press, 1992.

Colby, William. *Lost Victory: A Firsthand Account of America's Sixteen-Year Involvement in Vietnam*. Chicago-New York: Contemporary Books, 1989.

Collier, Thomas, and John Shy. "Revolutionary War." In *Makers of Modern Strategy : Military thought from Machiavelli to Hitler*, by G. A. Craig and F. Gilbert E. M. Earle, 456. Princeton, NJ: Princeton University Press., 1978.

Connable, Ben, and Martin C. Libicki. *How Insurgencies End*. Monograph Series. Santa Monica, CA: RAND Corporation, 2010.

Comber, Leon. *Malaya's Secret Police 1945-1960: The Role of the Special Branch in the Malayan Emergency*. Melbourne: Monash University Press, 2009.

Corum, James. *Training Indigenous Forces in Counterinsurgency: A Tale of Two Insurgencies*. Carlisle PA: Strategic Studies Institute, 2006.

Deery, Philip. "Malaya, 1948: Britain's Asian Cold War?" Working Paper, International Center for Advance Studies, New York University, April 2002.

De Tocqueville, Alexis. *Democracy in America*. New York: Penguin, 1956.

Freedman, Lawrence. *The Transformation of Strategic Affairs*. London: Routledge, 2006.

Friedman, Thomas. *The Lexus and the Olive Tree, Understanding Globalization*. New York: Anchor Books, 2000.

Galula, David. *Counterinsurgency Warfare: Theory and Practice*. Saint Petersburg, FL: Glenwood Press, 1964.

Gardner, Ina. *In Service of the Sultan*. London: Pen and Sword, 2007.

Geraghty,Tony. *Inside the SAS*. New York: Ballantine, 1982.

Goldwin, Robert A., and John Fitzgerald Kennedy. *Why Foreign Aid?* Manchester NH: Ayer Publishing, 1971.

Gomez Jr, Hilario. *The Moro Rebellion and the Search for Peace: A Study on Christian-Muslim Relations in the Philippines*. Zamboanga City, Philippines: Silsilah Publications, 2000.

Greem, T. N. *The Guerilla: Selections from the Marine Corps Gazzette*. New York: Praeger, 2005.

Gywnn, Major General Sir Charles W. *Imperial Policing.* London: MacMillian and Co., 1934.

Hack, Karl. "Screwing Down the People: The Malayan Emergency, Decolonisation and Ethnicity." In *Imperial Policy and Southeast Asian Nationalism*, edited by. H. Antlov and S. Tonnesson, 95. Richmond, UK: Curzon Press, 1995.

Halliday, Fred. *Arabia Without Sultans.* New York: Vintage Books, 1997.

Halperin, Morton H. *Bureaucratic Politics and Foreign Policy.* Washington, DC: The Brookings Institute, 1974.

Hatch, Mary Jo. *Organization Theory: Modern Symbolic and Postmodern Perspectives.* Oxford University Press, 1997.

Henniker, Brigadier M. C. A. *Red Shadow Over Malaya.* London: William Blackwood & Sons, 1955.

Hunt, Richard. *Pacification: The American Struggle for Vietnam's Hearts and Minds.* Boulder, CO: Westview Press, 1995.

Huber, Thomas M. "Napoleon in Spain and Naples: Fortified Compound Warfare." In *Compound Warfare: That Fatal Knot*, Edited by Thomas M. Huber. Fort Leavenworth, KS: United States Army Command and General Staff College Press, 2002.

Huntington, Samuel P. *The Soldier and The State: theory and Politics of Civil Military Realtions.* Cambridge, MA: The Belknap Press of Harvard University, 1957.

Jeapes, Tony. *SAS: Operation Oman.* London: William Kimber, 1980.

Jones, Seth. *Counterinsurgency in Afghanistan,* Rand Counterinsurgency Study, Vol. 4. Santa Monica, CA: RAND Corporation, 2008.

———. *In The Graveyard of Empires: America's War in Afghanistan.* New York: W. W. Norton & Company, 2009.

Joya, Malalai. *Raising My Voice: The Extraordinary Story of the Afghan Woman Who Dares to Speak Out.* London: Rider, 2000.

Jureidini, Paul A. *Case Studies in Isurgency and Revolutionary Warfare: Algeria 1954-1962.* Special Operations Research Office Case Study, Washington, DC: Special Operations Research Office, The American University, 1963.

Karnow, Stanley. *In Our Image:America's Empire in the Philippines.* New York: Ballantine Books, 1990.

Kelly, Francis J. *Vietnam Studies: U.S. Army Special Forces 1961-1971.* Washington, DC: Department of the Army, 1985.

Kessler, Richard. *Rebellion and Repression in the Philippines.* New Haven, CT: Yale University Press, 1991Kilcullen, David. *The Accidental Guerrilla : Fighting Small Wars in the Midst of a Big One.* New York: Oxford University Press., 2009.

Kitson, Frank. *Bunch of Five.* London: Faber and Faber, 1977.

———. *Low Intensity Operations: Subversion, Insurgency, Peacekeeping.* London: Archon Books, 1971.

Knoebl, Kuno. *Victor Charlie.* New York: Frederick A. Praegar Publishers, 1967.

Krepinevich, Andrew F. Jr. *The Army and Vietnam.* Baltimore: Johns Hopkins University Press, 1986.

Lipset, Seymour Martin. *Political Man: The Social Bases of Politics.* London: Heinemann Publishing, 1983.

Lundberg, Kristen. "The Accidental Statesman." *Kennedy School of Government Case Study Program,* 2008.

MacKinlay, John. *The Insurgent Archipelago : From Mao to Bin Laden.* New York: Columbia University Press, 2009.

Majid, Rahnema. *Quand la misère chasse la pauvreté.* Arles: Actes Sud, 2003.

Malkasian, Carter. "Counterinsurgency in Iraq." In *Counterinsurgency in Modern Warfare,* edited by Daniel Marston and Carter Malkasian, 287-210. Oxford: Osprey Publishing, 2010.

Malvesti, Michele. *Time for Action: Redefining SOF Missions and Activities.* Working Paper, Washington, DC: Center for a New American Security, December 2009.

Mao, Zedong. *On Guerrilla Warfare.* New York: Praeger, 1961.

———. *Selected Works, Vol. II.* New York: International Publishers, 1954.

Marston, Daniel. "Lost and Found in the Jungle." In *Big Wars and Small Wars,* edited by Hew Strachan, 96-114. London: Routledge, 2006.

———. "Realizing the Extent of Our Errors and Forging the Road Ahead: Afghanistan 2001-2010." In *Counterinsurgency in Modern Warfare,* edited by Daniel Marston and Carter Malkasian, 251-286. Oxford: Osprey Publishing, 2010.

Marston, Daniel, and Carter Malkasian. *Counterinsurgency in Modern Warfare.* Oxford: Osprey Publishing, 2008.

McCrystal, General Stanley. "Commander's Initial Assessment, August 2009."

McCuen,John. *The Art of Counter-Revolutionary War*. Harrisburg, PA: Stockpole Books, 1966.

McKenna, Thomas M. *Muslim Rulers and Rebels: Everyday Politics and Armed Separatism in the Southern Philippines*. Berkeley: University of California Press, 1998.

McNamara, Robert. *In Retrospect: The Tragedy and Lessons of Vietnam*. New York: Random House, 1995.

Miers, Richard. *Shoot To Kill*. London: Faber and Faber, 1959.

Mockaitis, Thomas R. *The "New" Terrorism: Myths and Reality*. Stanford, CA: Stanford University Press, 2008.

———. *Iraq and the Challenge of Counterinsurgency*. Westport, CT: Praeger Security International, 2008.

Moyar, Mark. *A Question of Command: Counterinsurgency from Civil War to Iraq*. New Haven, CT: Yale University Press, 2009.

———. *Afghanistan's New Interior Minister: A Potential Game Changer*. Washington, DC: Orbis Publications, 2010.

———. *Triumph Forsaken: The Vietnam War, 1954-1965*. New York: Cambridge University Press, 2006.

Murphy, Robert, James B. Pearson, and et al. *Commission on the Organization of the Government for the Conduct of Foreign Policy*. Congressional Commission, Washington, DC: Government Printing Office, June 1975.

Nagl, John A. *Counterinsurgency Lessons From Malaya and Vietnam: Learning to Eat Soup with a Knife*. Westport, CT: Praeger, 2002.

Nagl, John. "Counterinsurgency in Vietnam: American Organizational Culture and Learning." In *Counterinsurgency in Madern Warfare*, edited by Daniel Marston and Carter Makasian, 119-136. Oxford: Osprey Publishing, 2008.

National Intelligence Council. *Estimative Products on Vietnam 1948-1975*. Historical Collection, Pittsburgh PA: Government Printing Office, April 2005.

Niven, B. M. *Special Men and Special War–Portraits of the SAS and Dhofar*. Singapore: Imago Limited, 1990.

Nuzum, Henry. The Letort Papers. *Shades of CORDS in the Kush: The False Hope of "Unity of Effort" in American Counterinsurgency.* Carlisle, PA: Strategic Studies Institute, U.S. Army War College, 2010.

O'Neill, Bard. "Revolutionary War in Oman." In *Insurgency in the Modern World*, edited by Bard O'Neill, 213-234. Boulder, CO: Westview Press, 1980.

———. *Confronting the Hydra.* Sydney Australia: Lowy Institute, 2009.

Ongkili, James P. *Nation-building in Malaysia 1946–1974.* Singapore: Oxford University Press, 1985.

Paret, Peter. "Clausewitz." In *Makers of Modern Strategy: From Machiavelli to the Nuclear Age*, by Peter Paret, 186-217. Princeton: Princeton University Press, 1986.

———. *French Revolutionary Warfare from Indochina to Algeria: The Analysis of a Political and Military Doctrine.* London: Pall Mall Press, 1964.

Paget, Julian. *Counter-Insurgency Campaigning.* London: Faber Publishing, 1967.

Peterson, J. *Oman's Insurgencies: The Sultanate's Struggle for Supremacy.* London: SAQI, 2007.

Petraeus, David Howell. *The American Military and The Lessons of Vietnam: A Study of Military Influence and The Use of Force in The Post Vietnam Era.* Princeton, NJ: UMI, Ann Arbor Michigan, 1987.

Perkins, Kenneth. *A Fortunate Soldier.* London: Brasseys, 1988.

Purcell, Victor. *Malaya: Communist or Free?* Stanford, CA: Stanford University Press, 1954.

Race, Jeffrey. *War Comes to Long An.* Berkley, CA: University of California Press, 1972.

Santos Jr., Soliman M., and Paz Verdades M. Santos, *with* Octavio A. Dinampo, Herman Joseph S. Kraft, Artha Kira R. Paredes, and Raymund Jose G. Quilop, ed. Diana Rodriguez. *Primed and Purposeful: Armed Groups and Human Security Efforts in the Philippine. Executive Summary* (France: Natura Press, 2010).

Salman, Michael. *The Embarrassment of Slavery: Controversies over Bondage and Nationalism in the American Colonial Philippines.* Univerity of California Press, 2001.

Schirmer, Daniel B., and Stephen Rosskamm Shalom. *The Philippines Reader: A History of Colonialism, Neocolonialism, Dictatorship, and Resistance.* Cambridge, MA: South End Press, 1987.

Sheehan,Neil. *A Bright Shining Lie: John Paul Vann and America in Vietnam*. New York: Random House, 1988.

Short, Anthony. *The Communist Insurrection in Malaya*. Plymouth, NY: Frederick Muller, 1975.

Shy, John, and Thomas Collier. "Revolutionary war." In *Makers of Modern Strategy*, edited by Peter Paret, 815-862. 2001.

Smith, Rupert. *The Utility of Force: The Art of War in the Modern World*. New York: Knopf, 2007.

Sorley, Lewis. *Vietnam Chronicles: The Abrams Tapes 1968-1972*. Lubbock, TX: Texas Tech University Press, 2004.

Stubbs, Richard. "From Search and Destroy to Hearts and Minds: The Evolution of British Strategy in Malaya 1948-60." In *Counterinsurgency in Modern Warfare*, edited by Daniel Marston and Carter Malkasian, 101-118. Oxford: Osprey Publishing, 2010.

Sunderland, Riley. *Organizing Counterinsurgency in Malaya: 1947–1960*. Santa Monica, CA: RAND Corporation, 1964.

———. *Wining the Hearts and Minds of the People: Malaya, 1948-1960*. Santa Monica, CA: RAND Corp, 1964.

Taber, Robert. *The War of the Flea : A Study of Guerrilla Warfare Theory and Practice*. New York: L. Stuart, 1965.

Taylor, Maxwell. *Swords Into Ploughshares*.

Thompson, Robert. *Defeating Communist Insurgency*. London: Chatto and Windus, 1966.

Thompson, W. Scott, and Donaldson Frizzell. *The Lessons of Vietnam*. New York: Crane, Russak & Company, 1977.

Trinquier, Roger. *Modern Warfare: A French View of Counterinsurgency*. Westport, CT: Praego, 1964.

Ucko, David. *The New Counterinsurgency Era: Transforming the US Military for Modern Wars*. Washington, DC: Georgetown University Press, 2009.

Ulin, Robert. *Memoirs of The Cold War*. Fort Leavenworth, KS: Self published, 2010.

Weber, Max. *Economy and Society: An Outline of Interpretive Sociology*, Vol. 2. Berkley, CA: University of California Press, 1978.

Willbanks, James. *Abandoning Vietnam*. Lawrence, KS: University of Kansas Press, 2004.

Wilson, John Q. *Bureaucracy: What Government Agencies Do and Why They Do It?* New York: Basic Books, 1989.

Wolf, Charles Jr. *Insurgency and Counterinsurgency: New Myths and old Realities*. Santa Monica, CA: RAND Corporation, July 1965.

Woodward, Bob. *Obama's Wars*. New York: Simon & Schuster, 2010.

Wright, Donald P., and Timothy Reese. *On Point II*. Fort Leavenworth, KS: Combat Studies Institute, 2008.

Young, Marilyn B. *Counterinsurgency, Now and Forever and Lloyd C. Gardner, Iraq and the Lessons of Vietnam: Or, How Not to Learn from the Past*. New York: The New Press, 2007.

Periodicals

Afsar, Shahid and Chris Samples. "The Taliban: an organizational analysis." *Military Review* (May-June, 2008): 8.

Barno, David. "Fighting the other war: Counterinsurgency strategy in Afghanistan 2003-2005." *Military Review* (September-October 2007): 32-44.

Bennett, Huw. "The Other Side of the COIN: Minimum and Exemplary Force in British Army Counterinsurgency in Kenya." *Small Wars and Insurgencies* 18, no. 4 (December 2007): 638-64.

Bierly, Jerome F., and Timothy W. Pleasant. "Malaya-A Case Study." *Marine Corps Gazette* 74 (July 1990): 48.

Birtle, Andrew J. "PROVN, Westmoreland, and the Historians: A Reappraisal." *Journal of Military History* (2008): 1213-1246.

Bowden, Mark. "Manhunt." *The Atlantic* (March 2007): 54.

Burton, Brian, and John Nagl. "Learning as we go: the US Army adapts to COIN in Iraq, July 2004-December 2006." *Small Wars and Insurgencies* 19, no. 3 (September 2008): 303-327.

Castan, Sam. "Vietnam's Two Wars." *Look* (January 1964): 32-36.

Caslen, Robert L., Thomas P. Guthrie, and Gregory L. Boylan. "The Operations Targeting and Effects Synchronization Process in Northern Iraq." *Military Review* (May-June 2010): 29-37.

Chiarelli, Peter, and Patrick Michaelis. "The Requirements for Full-Spectrum Operations." *Military Review* (July-August 2005): 4-17.

Curry, Andrew. "Mathematics of Terror." *DISCOVER* (July/August 2010): 38.

Curry Demarest, Geoff. "Let's take the French Experience in Algeria Out of U.S. Counterinsurgency Doctrine." *Military Review* (July-August 2010): 19-24.

Dixon, Paul. "British Counter-Insurgency from Malaya to Iraq." *Journal of Strategic Studies,* 32, no.3 (2009): 353-381.

Echevarria, Antulio J. II. "The Trouble with History." *Parameters* (Summer 2005): 78-88.

Fitzsimmons, Michael. "Hard Hearts and Open Minds? Governance, Identity and the Intellectual Foundations of Counterinsurgency Strategy," *Journal of Strategic Studies* 31 (June 2008): 342-347.

Gentile, Gian. "A Strategy of Tactics: Population Centric COIN and the Army." *Parameters* (Autumn 2009): 5-17.

Hoffman, Frank. "Neo-Classical Counter-Insurgency?" *Parameters* (Summer 2007): 77-87.

Hosmer, Stephen T., and Sibylle O. Crane. "Counterinsurgency, A Symposium April 16-20, 1962." Washington, DC: RAND, 1962.

Jaffe, Greg, Scott Wilson, and Karen DeYoung. "U.S. Envoy Resists Increase in Troops." *Washington Post*, 12 November 2009.

Jones, David Martin, and M. L. R. Smith. "Whose Hearts and Whose Minds? The Curious Case of Global Counter-Insurgency." *The Journal of Strategic Studies* 33 (February 2010): 97.

Manea, Octavian. "Interview with Dr. John Nagl." *Small Wars Journal.* http://smallwars journal.com/blog/journal/docs-temp/599-manea.pdf (accessed 1 November 2010).

———. "Interview with Dr. David Kilcullen," *Small War Journal*, 8 November 2010, http://renekogutudartiklid.blogspot.com/2010/11/interview-with-dr-david-kilcullen.html (accessed 15 November 2010).

Lacquement, Richard. "Integrating Civilian and Military Activities." *Parameters* (March 2010): 20-33.

Ladwig, Walter III. "Supporting Allies in COIN: Britain and the Dhofar Rebellion." *Small Wars and Insurgencies* 19, no. 1 (March 2008): 62-88.

Lawrence, T.E., "Twenty-Seven Articles," *The Arab Bulletin.* (20 August 1917).

Lieven, Anatol. "The War in Afghanistan: Its Background and Future Prospects." *Conflict, Security and Development* 9, no. 3 (October 2009): 333-359.

Malkasian, Carter. "The Role of Perceptions and Political reform in Counterinsurgency: The Case of Western Iraq, 2004-2005." *Small Wars and Insurgencies* 17, no. 3 (September 2006): 367-394.

Markel, Wade. "Draining the Swamp: The British Strategy of Population Control." *Parameters* (Spring 2006): 35-48.

Marston, Daniel. "Adaptation in the Field: The British Army's Difficult Campaign in Iraq." *Security Challenges* 6, no. 1 (Autumn 2010): 71-78.

Partlow, Joshua. "Tensions Between Eikenberry, McChrystal will be focus of their Washington visit." *The Washington Post*, 9 May 2010.

Popplewell, R. "Lacking Intelligence:" Some Reflections on Recent Approaches to British Counterinsurgency, 1900-1960." *Intelligence and National Security* (April 1995), 337.

Rubin, Barnett and Ahmed Rashid. "The Great Game to the Great Bargain." *Foreign Affairs* 87, no. 6 (November/December 2008): 30-44.

Semple, Michael, and Fotini Christia. "How to flip the Taliban." *Foreign Affairs* (July/August 2009).

Sepp, Kalev PhD. "Best Practices in Counterinsurgency." *Military Review* (May-June 2005): 8-12.

Smith, Neil, and Colonel Sean MacFarland. "Anbar Awakens: The Tipping Point." *Military Review* (March/April 2008): 41-53.

Strachan, Hew. "British Counter-Insurgency from Malaya to Iraq." *Royal United Services Institute Journal* 152, no. 6 (December. 2007): 8.

Wilder, Andrew. "Weapons System Based on Wishful Thinking," *The Boston Globe,* (16 September 2009).

Wilson, Gregory. "Anatomy of Anatomy of a Successful COIN Operation: OEF-P and the Indirect Approach." *Military Review* (November-December 2006).

Government Documents

Ahern, Thomas L. *CIA and Rural Pacification in South Vietnam.* CIA History Report Classified Secret, Declassified in 2001, Langley, VA: CIA History Staff Center For The Study of Intelligence, 2001.

Army, British. *Counter Insurgency Operations (Strategic and Operational Guideleines) : Combined Arms Operations Part 10.* London, 2001.

British Document End of Empire (BDEE), *The Situation in Malaya.* Cabinet Memorandum, 1948.

Center for Army Lessons Learned. Handbook 09-27, *Commander's Guide to Money as a Weapon System Tactics, Techniques, and Procedures.* Fort Leavenworth, KS: Center for Army Lessons Learned April 2009.

———. *Provicial Reconstruction Teams: Tactics, Techniques, and Procedures.* Fort Leavenworth, KS: Combined Arms Center, 2007.

Department of the Army. Field Manual (FM) 3-0, *Operations.* Washington, DC: Government Printing Office, 2008.

———. Field Manual (FM) 3-24, *Counterinsurgency.* Washington, DC: Department of the Army, 2006.

Henriksen, Thomas H. "Afghanistan, Counterinsurgency, and the Indirect Approach," JSOU Report 10-3. Hurlburt Field, FL: Joint Special Operations University, 2010.

The Government White Paper Report, *The Militant Communist Threat to Malaysia.* Kuala Lumpur: National Press, 1966.

Joint Center for Operational Analysis. *Provicial Reconstruction Teams in Afghanistan: An Interagency Assessment.* Directed Assessment, Suffolk, Virgina: US Department of Defense, Joint Center for Operational Analysis, 2010.

Joint Chiefs of Staff. Joint Publication (JP) 1-02, *Department of Defense Dictionary of Military and Associated Terms.* Washington, DC: Department of Defense, 2010.

———. Joint Publication (JP) 3-0, *Joint Operations.* Washington, DC: Government Printing Office, 2008.

———. Joint Publication (JP) 3-05, *Doctrine for Joint Special Operations.* Washington, DC: Government Printing Office, 2003.

Land War Centre. "ARMY Field Manual Countering Insurgency." *British Army Field Manuals* (Ministry of Defence, United Kingdom) 1, no. 10 (January 2010).

Ministry of Defense. Joint Warfare Publication (JWP) 3-50, *Military Contributions to Peace Support Operations.* DSDA Operations Centre, 2004.

Noonan, Michael J. "A Mile Deep and an Inch Wide: Foreign Internal Defense Campaigning in Dhofar, Oman and El Salvador." *The US Army and the Interagency Process: Historical Perspectives.* Fort Leavenworth KS: Combat Studies Institute Press, 2008. 199-215.

Quadrenial Defense Review Independent Review Panel. *The QDR in Perspective: Meeting America's National Security Needs in the 21st Century.* Panel Report, Washington DC: Advance Copy Received from Paul Hughes USIP, 2010.

Rigden, Colonel I. A. (O.B.E.), British Army. "The British Approach to Counter-Insurgency: Myths, Realities, and Strategic Challenge." Strategy Research Project, US Army War College, Carlisle Barracks, PA, 2008.

Strategic Studies Department. *United States Special Operations Command (USSOCOM) Research Topic 2010.* Hurlburt, FL, Joint Special Operations University, 2009.

US Army. *Counterinsurgency and Contingency Operations Doctrine 1942-1976.* Washington, DC: Center of Military History, United States Army, 2007.

US Congress. House of Representatives. Hearing on U.S. Aid to Pakistan: Planning and Accountability. Committee on Oversight and Government Reform. Subcommittee on National Security and Foreign Affairs, 9 December 2009.

US Government, DOD, DOS, USAID. "US Government Counterinsurgency Guide." Washington, DC.

US Marine Corps. FMFM 8-2, *Counterinsurgency Operations.* Washington, DC: Department of the Navy, 1967.

———. FMFM-21, *Operations Against Guerilla Forces.* Washington, DC: Department of the Navy, 1962.

Internet

Atwood, J. Brian. "Elevating Development Assistance." *Prism* 1, no.3. http://www.ndu.edu/ press/elevating-development-assistance.html (accessed 17 November 2010).

Datu Jamal Ashley Abbas. "Bangsa Moro Conflict–Historical Antecedents and Present Impact." Speech delivered by at the University of the Philippines in Los Baños on 5 September 2000. http://jamalashley.wordpress.com/2007/04/17/bangsa-moro-conflict-historical-antecedents-and-present-impact/ (accessed 9 November 2010).

Dickinson, Elizabeth. "A Bright Shining Slogan How 'Hearts and Minds' Came to Be." *Foreign Policy* (September/October 2009). http://www.foreignpolicy.com/articles/2009/08/13/ a_bright_shining_slogan (accessed 10 October 2010).

Fitzsimmons, Michael. "Hard Hearts and Open Minds? Governance, Identity and the Intellectual Foundations of Counterinsurgency Strategy." Paper presented at the annual meeting of the ISA's 49th Annual Convention, Bridging Multiple Divides, Hilton San Francisco, CA, 26 March 2008. http://www.allacademic.com/meta/ p252066_index.html (accessed 22 November 2010).

Green, Dan. "The Other Surge." *Armed Forces Journal*. http://www.armedforces journal.com/2010/10/4771231 (accessed 24 November 2010).

Hallinan, Conn. "The Great Myth: Counterinsurgency." *Foreign Policy in Focus*, 22 July 2010, http://www.fpif.org/articles/the_great_myth_counterinsurgency (accessed 25-October 2010).

Heilprin, John. "Biden Warns of Failure in Afghanistan." *Fox News*, 25 February 2008. http://www.foxnews.com/wires/2008Feb25/0,4670,US AfghanistanBiden,00.html (accessed 16 November 2010).

Kilcullen, David. "Counterinsurgency in Iraq: Theory and Practice, 2007." Power point presentation, September 2007. http://usacac.army.mil/cac2/coin/.../ Dr_Kilcullen_COIN_Brief%28Sep07%29.ppt (accessed 15 October 2010).

———. "Counter-insurgency Redux." http://smallwarsjournal.com/documents/ kilcullen1.pdf (accessed 5 November 2010).

Komer, Robert. "The Malayan Emergency in Retrospect: Organization of a Successful Counterinsurgency Effort." Report, Advanced Research Projects Agency, RAND Corporation, Santa Monica, CA, 1972. http://www.rand.org/ pubs/reports/R957/ (accessed 20 November 2010).

Kritz, Benjamin D. "US Policy Led to Dispute Between Muslims, Philippine Government." http://www.suite101.com/content/moro-rebellion-in-the-philippines-a63449 (accessed 10 November 2010).

Madge Kho. "The Bates Treaty " http://www.philippineupdate.com/Bates.htm (accessed 8 October 2010).

Manea, Octavian. "Interview with Dr. David Kilcullen." *Small War Journal*, 8 November 2010. http://renekogutudartiklid.blogspot.com/2010/11/interview-with-dr-david-kilcullen.html (accessed 15 November 2010).

McChrystal, GEN Stanley A. ISAF Commander's Counterinsurgency Guidance. http://www.isaf.nato.int/article/news/isaf-commanders-counterinsurgency-guidance.html (accessed 1 November 2010).

Minister of Home Affairs, Malaysia. The Government White Paper Report, "The Militant Communist Threat to Malaysia." 24 October 1966. www.digitalibrary.my/.../ malaysiakini/199_the%20militant%20communist%20threat%20to%20west%20m alaysia.pdf (accessed 5 November 2010)

Mulrine, Anna. "A Dangerous Backslide, Age-old Problems-and a new Taliban Surge-are Dragging the Afghans Down." *US News*, 8 October 2006. http://www.usnews.com/ usnews/news/articles/061008/16afghan.htm (accessed 15 November 2010).

Petraeus, GEN David. COMISAF Counterinsurgency Guidance Memorandum to ISAF Forces. 1 August 2010. http://www.isaf.nato.int/article/caat-anaysis-news/comisaf-coin-guidance.html (accessed 1 November 2010).

Transparency International. "Corruption Perception Index 2010 Results." http://www. transparency.org/policy_research/surveys_indices/cpi/2010/results (accessed 1 November 2010).

Turse, Nick. "Publish or Perish: Getting a read on The American War." *Huffington Post*, 14 October 2010, http://www.huffingtonpost.com/nick-turse/publish-or-perish-getting_b_762678.html?view=print (accessed 10 November 2010).

Wilder, Andrew. "Winning Hearts and Minds?" NPR, 4 April 2010. http://npr.vo.llnwd.net/ kip0/_pxn=0+_pxK=17273/anon.nprmp3/npr/me/ 2009/11/20091104_me_02.mp3?dl=1 (accessed 16 November 2011).

Interviews

Command and General Staff College (CGSC) Scholars Program 2010. *Scholars Program Counterinsurgency Research Study 2010.* Research Study, Fort Leavenworth, KS: Ike Skelton Chair in Counterinsurgency, 2010. This study included over 80 interviews of counterinsurgency practitioners and policy professionals from the United States and United Kingdom. All interviews are held with the Ike Skelton Chair in Counterinsurgency, CGSC Fort Leavenworth Kansas.

Fort Bragg, North Carolina

AA601, Battalion Commander. Interview by Michael Dinesman and Winston Marbella, 13-24 August 2010.

AA602, Civil Affairs Company Commander. Interview by Michael Dinesman and Winston Marbella, 13-24 August 2010.

AA603, Civil Affairs Team Leader. Interview by Michael Dinesman and Winston Marbella, 13-24 August 2010.

AA604, Civil Affairs Team Leader. Interview by Michael Dinesman and Winston Marbella, 24 August 2010.

AA605, Civil Affairs First Sergeant. Interview by Michael Dinesman and Winston Marbella, 24 August 2010.

AA606, Company Commander. Interviewed by Travis Molliere and Carrie Przelski, 20 August 2010.

AA607, Special Forces Commander. Interview by Travis Molliere and Carrie Przelski, 27 August 2010.

AA608, Battalion Commander. Interview by Travis Molliere and Carrie Przelski, 23 August 2010.

AA609, Brigade Commader. Interview by Travis Molliere and Carrie Przelski, 17 August 2010.

AA610, Division Staff Officer. Interview by Travis Molliere and Carrie Przelski, 17 August 2010.

AA611, Platoon Sergeant. Interview by Travis Molliere and Carrie Przelski, 23 August 2010.

AA612, Psychological Operations Officer. Interview by travis Molliere and Carrie Przelski, 20 August 2010.

AA613, Logistics Advisor. Interview by Travis Molliere and Carrie Przelski, 16 August 2010.

AA614, Advise and Assist Battalion Commander. Interview by Travis Molliere and Carrie Przelski, 19 August 2010.

AA615, Psychological Operations Planner. Interview by Travis Molliere and Carrie Przelski, 23 August 2010.

AA616, Assistant S4. Interview by Travis Molliere and Carrie Przelski, 16 August 2010.

AA617, Platoon Leader. Interview by Travis Molliere and Carrie Przelski, 16 August 2010.

AA618, Special Forces Commander. Interview by Michael Dinesman and Winston Marbella, 31 August 2010.

AA619, Special Forces Company Commander. Interview by Michael Dinesman and Winston Marbella, 31 August 2010.

AA620, Special Forces Company Commander. Interview by Michael Dinesman and Winston Marbella, 2 September 2010.

AA621, Special Forces Officer. Interview by Michael Dinesman, 3 September 2010.

AA622, Special Forces Warrant Officer, Interview by Michael Dinesman and Winston Marbella, 2 September 2010.

AA623, Civil Affairs Company Commander. Interview by Michael Dinesman and Winston Marbella, 23 August 2010.

AA624, Special Forces ODA Commander. Interview by Michael Dinesman and Winston Marbella, 1 September 2010.

AA625, Special Forces ODA Commander. Interview by Michael Dinesman and Winston Marbella, 1 September 2010.

Fort Carson, Colorado

Ranger Company Commander. Interview by Jesse Stewart and Brian McCarthy, 24-27 August 2010, AA301.

Special Forces Company Commander. Interview by Jesse Stewart and Brian McCarthy, 24-27 August 2010, AA302.

Special Forces Commander. Interview by Jesse Stewart and Brian McCarthy, 24-27 August 2010, AA303.

Company Commander. Interview by Jesse Stewart and Brian McCarthy, 24-27 August 2010, AA304.

Special Forces Commander. Interview by Jesse Stewart and Brian McCarthy, 24-27 August 2010, AA305.

Special Forces Operations Officer. Interview by Jesse Stewart and Brian McCarthy, 24-27 August 2010, AA306.

Special Forces Company Commander. Interview by Jesse Stewart and Brian McCarthy, 24-27 August 2010, AA307.

Battalion S3. Interview by Jesse Stewart and Brian McCarthy, 24-27 August 2010, AA308.

Battalion S3. Interview by Jesse Stewart and Brian McCarthy, 24-27 August 2010, AA309.

Company Commander. Interview by Jesse Stewart and Brian McCarthy, 24-27 August 2010, AA310.

Fort Drum, New York

AA201, Brigade Commander. Interview by Jan K. Gleiman and Michael Dinesman, 17-20 August 2010.

AA202, Brigade Planner. Interview by Jan K. Gleiman and Michael Dinesman, 17-20 August 2010.

AA203, Command Sergeant Major. Interview by Jan K. Gleiman and Michael Dinesman, 17-20 August 2010.

AA204, Battalion S3. Interview by Jan K. Gleiman and Michael Dinesman, 17-20 August 2010.

AA205, Company Commander. Interview by Jan K. Gleiman and Michael Dinesman, 17-20 August 2010.

AA206, Troop Commander. Interview by Jan K. Gleiman and Michael Dinesman, 17-20 August 2010.

AA207, Company Commander. Interview by Jan K. Gleiman and Michael Dinesman, 17-20 August 2010.

AA208, Artillery Platoon Leader. Interview by Jan K. Gleiman and Michael Dinesman, 17-20 August 2010.

AA209, Scout Platoon Leader. Interview by Jan K. Gleiman and Michael Dinesman, 17-20 August 2010.

Fort Riley, Kansas

AA101, Sergeant Major. Interview by Jesse Stewart and Brian McCarthy, 15-19 August 2010.

AA102, Company First Sergeant. Interview by Jesse Stewart and Brian McCarthy, 15-19 August 2010.

AA103, Brigade Commander. Interview by Jesse Stewart and Brian McCarthy, 15-19 August 2010.

AA104, Battalion S3. Interview by Jesse Stewart and Brian McCarthy, 15-19 August 2010.

AA105, Company Commander. Interview by Jesse Stewart and Brian McCarthy, 15-19 August 2010.

AA106, Support Battalion Commander. Interview by Jesse Stewart and Brian McCarthy, 15-19 August 2010.

AA107, Battalion Commander. Interview by Jesse Stewart and Brian McCarthy, 15-19 August 2010.

AA108, Battalion Command Sergeant Major. Interview by Jesse Stewart and Brian McCarthy, 15-19 August 2010.

AA109, Platoon Sergeant. Interview by Jesse Stewart and Brian McCarthy, 15-19 August 2010.

AA110, Battalion Executive Officer and S3. Interview by Jesse Stewart and Brian McCarthy, 15-19 August 2010.

AA111, Psychological Operations Company Commander. Interview by Jesse Stewart and Brian McCarthy, 15-19 August 2010.

Fort Leavenworth, Kansas

AA501, Brigade Executive Officer. Interview by Jan K. Gleiman and Karsten Haake, 1 September 2010.

AA502, Division Aide-de-Camp. Interview by Jan K. Gleiman and Karsten Haake, 7 September 2010.

AA503, Aviation Planner marine Corps. Interview by Jan K. Gleiman and Karsten Haake, 1 September 2010.

AA504, Military Police Company Commander. Interview by Jan K. Gleiman and Kasten Haake, 1 September 2010.

AA505, Director USA Counterinsurgency Center. Interview by Winston Marbella and Michael Dinesman, 1 August 2010.

AA506, Division Chief of Staff. Interview by Brian McCarthy and Jesse Stewart, 3 August 2010.

AA507, Special Forces Commander. Interview by Michael Dinesman and Winston Marbella, 12 August 2010.

AA508, Senior Advisor to Iraqi Army. Interview by Karsten Haake and Winston Marbella, 17 August 2010.

AA509, Division Commander. Interview by Jan K. Gleiman and Karsten Haake, 25 August 2010.

AA510, Division Chief of Staff. Interview by Travis Molliere and Jesse Stewart, 12 August 2010.

AA512, Colonel (Retired) Roger Donlon. Interview by Jan K. Gleiman and Brian McCarthy, 6 August 2010.

AA513, Border Transition Team Commander. Interview by Michael Dinesman, 25 October 2010.

AA514, Haseman, John. Interview by Jan K. Gleiman and Winston Marbella, 8 September 2010.

Fort Lewis, Washington

AA401, Battalion Commander. Interview by Jesse Stewart and Brian McCarthy, 30 August-3 September 2010.

AA402, Special Forces Commander. Interview by Jesse Stewart and Brian McCarthy, 30August-3 September 2010.

AA403, Battalion S3. Interview by Jesse Stewart and Brian McCarthy, 30 August-3 September 2010.

Marine Corps Base Quantico, Virginia

AA901, Police Transition Team Advisor. Interview by Karsten Haake and Jan K. Gleiman, 17 September 2010.

AA902, Police Transition Team Advisor. Interview by Karsten Haake and Jan K. Gleiman, 17 September 2010.

AA903, Company Executive Officer. Interview by Brian McCarthy and Carrie Przelski, 17 Sepetember 2010.

AA904, Logistics Advisor. Interview by Jan K. Gleiman and Karsten Haake, 17 September 2010.

AA905, Company Executive Officer. Interview by Michael Dinesman and Winston Marbella, 17 September 2010.

AA906, Transition Team Advisor. Interview by Brian McCarthy and Michael Dinesman, 17 September 2010.

AA907, Battalion Commander. Interview by Jan K. Gleiman and Karsten Haake, 17 September 2010.

United Kingdom

AA1001, Noncommissioned officer Panel 4 Rifles. Interview by Brian McCarthy, Jan K. Gleiman, and Travis Molliere, 28 September 2010.

AA1002, British Platoon Commander. Interview by Brian McCarthy and Winston Marbella, 1 October 2010.

AA1003, British Battalion S2. Interview by Travis Molliere and Carrie Przelski, 1 October 2010.

AA1004, British Regimental Commander. Interview by Jesse Stewart and Brian McCarthy, 26 September 2010.

AA1005, Dhofar Veterans Panel. Interview by Jan K. Gleiman, Brian McCarthy, Travis Molliere, Karsten Haake, Carrie Przelski, and Winston Marbella, 29 September 2010.

AA1006, Retired British General Officer. Interview by Jan K. Gleiman, Carrie Przelski, and Michael Dinesman, 27 September 2010.

AA1007, Platoon Leader, Interview by Jan K. Gleiman and Brian McCarthy, 29 September 2010.

AA1008, British Task Force Chief of Staff. Interview by Brian Mccarthy and Michael Dinesman, 7 October 2010.

AA1009, General Sir Frank Kitson BA (Retired). Interview by Jan K. Gleiman, Brian McCarthy, Carrie Przelski, Travis Molliere, 4 October 2010.

AA1010, Battlion Commander. Interview by Jan K. Gleiman and Michael Dinesman, 7 October 2010.

AA1011, British General Officer. Interviewed by Jan K. Gleiman, Brian McCarthy, and Michael Dinesman, 29 September 2010.

AA1012, British General Officer. Interviewed by Jan K. Gleiman, Brian McCarthy, Jesse Stewart,and Michael Dinesman, 22 September 2010.

AA1013, British General Officer. Interviewed by Jan K. Gleiman, Brian McCarthy, Travis Molliere, Karsten Haake, Carrie Przelski, and Michael Dinesman, 23 September 2010.

AA1014, British Battalion Executive Officer. Interviewed by Jan K. Gleiman and Michael Dinesman, 29 September 2010.

AA1015, British Platoon Leader. Interviewed by Jan K. Gleiman and Brian McCarthy, 1 October 2010.

AA1016, Dr. John MacKinlay. Interviewed by Jan K. Gleiman, Brian McCarthy, Carrie Przelski, Michael Dinesman, 8 October 2010.

AA1017, Major General Tony Jeapes BA (Retired). Interviewed by Jan K. Gleiman, Michael Dinesman, Winston Marbella, and Carrie Przelski, 4 October 2010.

Washington, DC

AA801, Retired US Ambassador. Interview by Jan K. Gleiman, Michael Dinesman, Karsten Haake, Brian McCarthy, Winston Marbella, Travis Molliere, Jesse Stewart and Carrie Przelski, 13 September 2010.

AA802, Colette Rausch. Interview by Jan K. Gleiman and Winston Marbella, 15 September 2010.

AA803, Foreign Service Officer. Interview by Brian McCarthy and Jesse Stewart, 14 September 2010.

AA804, USAID Officer. Interview by Jan K. Gleiman and Karsten Haake, 14 September 2010.

AA805, Dr. Bernard Finel. Interview by Jesse Stewart, Carrie Przelski, and Brian McCarthy, 14 September 2010.

AA806, Policy Advisor. Interview by Jan K. Gleiman, Michael Dinesman, Karsten Haake, Brian McCarthy, Winston Marbella, Travis Molliere, Jesse Stewart, and Carrie Przelski, 13 September 2010.

AA807, Retired General Officer. Interview by Jesse Stewart and Jan K. Gleiman, 18 September 2010.

AA808, National Security Staff. Interview by Jan K. Gleiman, Karsten Haake, Carrie Przelski, and Winston Marbella, 15 September 2010.

AA809, Foreign Service Officer USAID. Interview by Michael Dinesman and Winston Marbella, 14 September 2010.

AA810, Action Officer Joint Staff. Interview by Jan K. Gleiman, Winston Marbella, Brian McCarthy and Travis Molliere, 13 September 2010.

AA811, Paul Hughes. Interview by Jan K. Gleiman, Winston Marbella, Carrie Przelski, and Karsten Haake, 15 September 2010.

AA812, Staffer ASD SOLIC. Interview by Jesse Stewart, Brian McCarthy, and Travis Molliere, 15 September 2010.

Lectures/ Presentations

Egnell, Robert. "Winning Legitimacy: A Critical Analysis of Hearts and Minds Approaches in Afghanistan." Paper presented at the annual meeting of the Theory vs. Policy? Connecting Scholars and Practitioners, New Orleans Hilton Riverside Hotel, The Loews New Orleans Hotel, New Orleans, LA, 17 February 2010.

Gambastes, Donald. "How Good Is Our System For Curbing Contract Fraud,Waste, And Abuse?" Testimony beforeThe Commission on Wartime Contracting in Iraq and Afghanistan, Washington, DC: United States Agency for International Development, 24 May 2010.

Lansdale, Edward G. "Counter-Guerilla Operations in the Philippines 1946-1953." Seminar held at Ft. Bragg, NC, June 1961.

CPSIA information can be obtained
at www.ICGtesting.com
Printed in the USA
LVHW061542110122
708310LV00012B/1270